THE T...
COMMANDMEN...

THE TEN COMMANDMENTS

The Master Key to Life

EMMET FOX

HarperOne
An Imprint of HarperCollinsPublishers

HarperOne

HarperCollins books may be purchased for educational, business, or sales promotional use. For information, please e-mail the Special Markets Department at SPsales@harpercollins.com.

HarperCollins Web site: http://www.harpercollins.com

HarperCollins®, 👑®, and HarperOne™ are trademarks of HarperCollins Publishers.

FIRST HARPERCOLLINS PAPERBACK EDITION PUBLISHED IN 1993

Library of Congress Cataloging-in-Publication Data

Fox, Emmet.
   The Ten commandments : the master key to life /
Emmet Fox.
   p. cm.
Originally published: New York : Harper & Row, 1953.
ISBN: 978–0–06–250307–7
1. Ten commandments—Sermons.   2. Sermons, American.
3. New Thought.   I. Title.
BV4655.F69   1993
241.5's—dc20   92–54664

HB 11.07.2022

Contents

Contents

Foreword

D R. Emmet Fox, the modern mystic, has the knack of taking profound spiritual truths and explaining them in a simple way so that all can understand and use them in their daily lives. Under his inspired handling the Bible comes to life, and what was sometimes dull and uninteresting or obscure suddenly takes on new and vivid meaning. There have been many people whose lives have been filled with new beauty and interest and joy through his inspired words.

Consequently, there has long been a demand for copies of his sermons and lectures by Bible students and seekers of Truth who have received healing and help through them. Indeed, in response to this insistent demand, Dr. Fox promised to put into book form especially his interpretation of the Ten Commandments, and the present volume fulfills that promise. It represents a series of sermons that were delivered to many thousands of persons in the Manhattan Opera House, New York City. Nothing has been changed and nothing has been deleted but the normal repetition that is necessary and desirable in the spoken word, but that in the written word becomes useless redundancy.

The Ten Commandments, as Moses gave them, set the stage for the rest of the Bible, and when spiritually understood form a master key to the Bible and to life. There is no problem that cannot be solved, nor any aspiration that cannot be fulfilled when once the underlying meaning is absorbed and made a part of one's life.

God is always ready when we are, and in this book Dr. Emmet Fox shows how to get that divine contact that will bring a freshness and newness to every department of your life.

HERMAN WOLHORN

THE TEN COMMANDMENTS

*A*nd Moses went down from the mount unto the people, and sanctified the people; and they washed their clothes.

And he said unto the people, Be ready against the third day: come not at your wives.

And it came to pass on the third day in the morning, that there were thunders and lightnings, and a thick cloud upon the mount, and the voice of the trumpet exceeding loud; so that all the people that was in the camp trembled.

And Moses brought forth the people out of the camp to meet with God; and they stood at the nether part of the mount.

And mount Sinai was altogether on a smoke, because the Lord descended upon it in fire: and the smoke thereof as cended as the smoke of a furnace, and the whole mount quaked greatly.

And when the voice of the trumpet sounded long, and waxed louder and louder, Moses spake, and God answered him by a voice.

And the Lord came down upon mount Sinai, on the top of the mount: and the Lord called Moses up to the top of the mount; and Moses went up.

And the Lord said unto Moses, Go down, charge the people, lest they break through unto the Lord to gaze, and many of them perish.

And let the priests also, which come near to the Lord, sanctify themselves, lest the Lord break forth upon them.

And Moses said unto the Lord, The people cannot come up to mount Sinai: for thou chargedst us, saying, Set bounds about the mount, and sanctify it.

And the Lord said unto him, Away, get thee down, and thou shalt come up, thou, and Aaron with thee: but let not the priests and the people break through to come up unto the Lord, lest he break forth upon them.

EXODUS 19:14–25

*A*nd God spake all these words, saying,
   I am the Lord thy God, which have brought thee out of the land of Egypt, out of the house of bondage.

   Thou shalt have no other gods before me.

   Thou shalt not make unto thee any graven image, or any likeness of anything that is in heaven above, or that is in the earth beneath, or that is in the water under the earth:

   Thou shalt not bow down thyself to them, nor serve them: for I the Lord thy God am a jealous God, visiting the iniquity of the fathers upon the children unto the third and fourth generation of them that hate me;

   And shewing mercy unto thousands of them that love me, and keep my commandments.

   Thou shalt not take the name of the Lord thy God in vain; for the Lord will not hold him guiltless that taketh his name in vain.

   Remember the sabbath day, to keep it holy.

   Six days shalt thou labour, and do all thy work:

   But the seventh day is the sabbath of the Lord thy God: in it thou shalt not do any work, thou, nor thy son, nor thy daughter, thy manservant, nor thy maidservant, nor thy cattle, nor thy stranger that is within thy gates:

   For in six days the Lord made heaven and earth, the sea, and all that in them is, and rested the seventh day: wherefore the Lord blessed the sabbath day, and hallowed it.

   Honour thy father and thy mother: that thy days may be long upon the land which the Lord thy God giveth thee.

   Thou shalt not kill.

   Thou shalt not commit adultery.

   Thou shalt not steal.

   Thou shalt not bear false witness against thy neighbor.

   Thou shalt not covet thy neighbour's house, thou shalt not covet thy neighbour's wife, nor his manservant, nor his maidservant, nor his ox, nor his ass, nor any thing that is thy neighbour's.

And all the people saw the thunderings, and the lightnings, and the noise of the trumpet, and the mountain smoking: and when the people saw it, they removed, and stood afar off.

And they said unto Moses, Speak thou with us, and we will hear: but let not God speak with us, lest we die.

And Moses said unto the people, Fear not: for God is come to prove you, and that his fear may be before your faces, that ye sin not.

And the people stood afar off, and Moses drew near unto the thick darkness where God was.

And the Lord said unto Moses, Thus thou shalt say unto the children of Israel, Ye have seen that I have talked with you from heaven.

Ye shall not make with me gods of silver, neither shall ye make unto you gods of gold.

EXODUS 20:1–22

CHAPTER 1

What Moses Means Today

W E are considering one of the most important sections in the Bible, a section that is certainly not neglected, because the Ten Commandments are taught everywhere, in Sunday schools and day schools, and often are written up on the walls of many churches. They are not neglected but they are woefully misunderstood.

It is still true today that the people stand afar off from the thick darkness where God is, but I am glad to say that that darkness is rapidly passing away. All over the world the main body of the people are getting the Truth about the Omnipresence and Availability of God. They do not call it that as a rule. However, they are learning and beginning to feel that God is something that we have with us every day, in the most prosaic and ordinary things. God is not just an abstract idea up in the sky, having no meaning in everyday life. That concept is going. All kinds of people, all over the world, are beginning to get the sense of God as a present, dynamic, real power for harmony, for healing, and for freedom.

There is nothing in the world more thrilling than the Bible, particularly our Bible in English. There is no literature in the world that comes within a thousand miles of it for literary power, for graphic presentation, for dramatic expression, for knowledge of human nature, and for human psychology, as it is the fashion at the moment, to call it. Yet I wonder how many people have read these two chapters, let us say, within the past year. How many would be astonished at the tremendous drama and human psychology they would find there, if they would read them.

Books and magazines and articles, alleged to be psychology, are pouring off the presses. The very word *psychology* would sell an old sin at the present time. Yet here at home on the shelf, in the Bible, is the most powerful, practical psychology ever written.

The book of Exodus, part of chapters 19 and 20, is not only one of the most important sections of the Bible, but also one of the most dramatic. I call it a section because it is part of two chapters that belong together. The chaptering in the Bible is not logical. The chapters, as we have them, were not made by the authors, but at a much later date—later than the Middle Ages. The authors knew nothing about our chapters. The works of these men were cut up for convenience in handling and reading, just as you might take a long ribbon and a pair of scissors and snip the ribbon off into separate yards. The verses also are quite modern. They were made somewhere about the beginning of the seventeenth century. And, of course, they are a very convenient device for reference.

Now, this section deals with what we call the Ten Commandments, and is one of the key sections of the Bible. The Sermon on the Mount is another, and the first two or three chapters of Genesis are another.

This section really sums up the whole Bible teaching. If we thoroughly understand it, then we have the gist of the whole Bible. We have the underlying principle that we can apply to understanding any part of the Bible, and that is the scientific way to approach the Bible.

It is one of the most important sections for us because it teaches us the laws of life, and it is only when we understand the laws of life that we become masters—masters of our own conditions. Divine Providence means us to be masters of our conditions.

It is sad to think how much goodwill and hard work have gone into Bible study in the past with so little result. I have known people who worked like Trojans on their Bible, not for a year, but for forty or fifty years, and at the end of that time they did not have the slightest inkling of the real Bible message. They were nearly all rigid fundamentalists. They missed the whole beauty of the Bible. They just took it literally, and were left at the end of their Bible study with what they had started with, and nothing more. They started with the belief in a rather terrible, very severe, limited God, Jehovah, Who was going to save a few people and send the rest to eternal torment; and they finished up with that, after literally learning the Bible by heart.

But in this section we get the underlying principle for understanding the whole Bible.

To begin with, notice which book it comes in. This extraordinary treatise on human nature and how it works, and how to find God, does not come in the book of Genesis or Numbers or Proverbs. It comes in Exodus. What does the word *Exodus* mean? It means an exit, a going or a getting out—getting out of trouble.

An exit is a way out, and, with trouble, the idea is to get out quickly. The book of Exodus deals with the getting out of limitation, which means the getting out of evil, because all evil is limitation of one kind or another. It shows us how to get out of our own limitation—our weakness, and fearfulness, and stupidity, and sin, and sickness—and become the wonderful thing that God intended us to be.

The Bible says that we have dominion over all things—and we have—but we can only have that dominion when we learn the laws of life and apply them. There is no dominion without it.

For instance, we are, to a large extent, masters of electricity today because in the past we studied the laws of electricity and applied them. Men like Edison, Marconi, Ampere, and Faraday did not sit down and hatch up some dream out of their own minds. No, Faraday, for example, got bits of wire and magnets, and twirled them about, and studied their action and learned the laws governing them.

We have the automobile today because people like Boyle studied the action of gases, and what happened with compression and expansion. And this knowledge was applied by people like Benz and others. They studied the laws appertaining to these conditions, and applied them. The result is that for a comparatively small sum today you can get a vehicle that Julius Caesar could not have got for the whole Roman Empire.

So if we want health, if we want happiness, if we want true self-expression, if we want divine freedom, then we have to learn the laws of the human soul, and the laws of psychology and metaphysics. We have to learn them and apply them—simplicity itself. Not easy, but simple.

These laws are explained in the Bible.

The Bible was written by men who had extraordinary knowledge of these laws. They got it through inspiration—as we can when we know how.

Moses in particular knew these laws extremely well. He was one of the greatest souls who has ever come upon the earth planet. He was a man of extraordinary understanding and knowledge of God and of man. He was born with that potentiality, having earned it when he had been on earth before. Then he was born again into the conditions that enabled him to use and develop those faculties. Just as a person today, who is doing his very best to gain a knowledge of God—not for any ulterior motive but for its own sake—a person who is trying to understand God, and life, and what he is here for, and trying to live as well as he can; the next time he comes here he will be born into circumstances that will give him every opportunity of getting a much fuller and higher knowledge early in life.

Moses had done that, and so he came into the world where he could best develop and do a useful work, where he could be useful to people—because we are not developing unless we are useful. We do not get spiritual development by going off by ourselves and saying, "I will save my own soul, and the rest of the world can go hang." That does not give any kind of spiritual development. It will merely make you unhappy and self-centered. In order to develop spiritually you must be doing something useful for other people, something unselfish. In the old phrase, you must be doing your duty in the state of life in which you happen to be called. No spiritual development will ever come with neglect of duty. What we call our duty—and *is* our duty—is the opportunity to express the spiritual understanding we have, and thereby to get more.

Moses, of course, is one of the great historical leaders of the human race. He is one of those people who have really made history, and the story of his birth is extremely important and significant, spiritually as well as materially.

You know the story. He was born in Egypt, which was in those days the most highly civilized place in the world. But at the time, the authorities gave orders to kill the male children. Well, Moses was born and his mother tried to save his life by placing him in a little basket. Pharaoh's daughter—the king's daughter—used to go down to the riverbank to bathe every day at a certain time. And they hid this little basket—they had made it and topped it with pitch—and they put it there where Pharaoh's daughter could not help but see it. And the sister of Moses was told to hide in among the tall reeds there by the banks of the Nile, to see what would happen.

Well, the king's daughter went into the river, and she saw this little basket, and she opened it, and the child cried. Being human her heart was touched. Who could resist the cry of a small child? She immediately looked around, and out came the sister; and you know the rest of the story, how the sister was sent to fetch a woman to take care of the child, and she brought Moses' own mother.

Now there is one remarkable text here. Pharaoh's daughter says to the woman: "Take this child, and nurse it, and I will give thee thy wages." You are Pharaoh's daughter, you know. You probably did not know it but you are. In the Bible sense you are Pharaoh's daughter as soon as you become interested in metaphysics, as soon as you reach out for the Christ truth. At that point you are Pharaoh's daughter. You are saving the infant Moses. The infant Moses here is that higher thing in you that draws you to this teaching, to this Truth. And so you take the child and nurse it and bring it up. What leads you to do that? The power of God in you.

We do not go to God. God brings us to Himself. "You would not have sought Me had you not already found

Me." "We love Him because He first loved us." It is the power of God in you that is doing it. God gives you the spiritual idea and says to you, "Take this child."

It is a baby, you know. When we get the spiritual idea it is a baby. When it grows up with us we will not be here any longer. We could not live on this plane. As soon as the spiritual idea grows up in us we will go and never come back—we have moved from the kindergarten up to high school.

But it is a baby, like the Christ child born in the stable, another way of putting the story of the Wonder Child.* So God gives us this child. It is feeble and it is crying, and He says to you and to me, "Take this child, and nurse it, and I will give thee thy wages." We have to nurse the infant Moses. We have to nurse the Christ child.

Now, how do we nurse a child? By giving it nourishment. And how do we nourish the infant Moses? By prayer and meditation. Otherwise the child will starve, and our chance for spiritual development will be gone for a long time. It will come again, but not for a long time. The child will starve. However, if we take the child and nurse it, we shall get our wages, and our wages shall be freedom, peace of mind, harmony, true place, understanding, and the fellowship of God Himself. These are the wages of prayer. Of course, we know the wages of sin is death.

And so the Bible says, "Take this child, and nurse it." There is really nothing else we can do for a baby but nurse it. The cleverest doctor who ever lived could not turn a small baby into a grown-up man in three months. All you can do is nurse it, and that is all you can do for the infant Moses. Nourish it. You nourish it with your daily

---

* See "The Wonder Child" in *Power Through Constructive Thinking* (Harper & Brothers), p. 1.

prayer and meditation and by the right thought all day long, not fussily pouncing on every thought, but by knowing in a general way that the Presence of God is with you, and refusing to give power to error. Take this child and nurse it and God will give you your wages.

The king's daughter adopted this child, we are told in this version, and Moses grew up as the adopted son of the king's daughter. That meant that he was one of the most important people in the kingdom.

Now, of course, according to modern ideas, the fact that he was adopted did not make him of royal blood—but those are modern ideas. What one might call the pure studbook of royalty or aristocracy belongs to Europe of the Middle Ages and since. The people in the ancient world did not take that point of view. In the Roman Empire, for instance, a man who was adopted was considered to have the blood of those who adopted him. And so also in the East. In the Roman Empire various distinctions of nationality did not mean anything. In modern Europe, since the Middle Ages, nationality has meant so much that it has finished up by practically destroying itself.

We have quite a national feeling in America, but not in that narrow-spirited way they had in Europe. In every country up to the outbreak of the last war you had to belong to that nation or you were very much a foreigner—French in France, German in Germany, Italian in Italy, British in England. If not, well then you were a foreigner and while you might be perfectly all right and no doubt meant well, and so forth, there was a difference. We do not feel that way in America. In America if a man is a good citizen we do not ask whether he spells his name Charles, Carl, or Carlos, but in Europe they had a different idea.

So Moses, having been adopted by the king's daughter, had every possible privilege, as though he were the king's actual grandson; and, as a matter of fact, many people have always thought that he was. Well, he was brought up and educated along Egyptian lines and he joined the priesthood. In the ancient world, if you wanted to amount to anything you had to be either a soldier or an ecclesiastic. The ancient world did not very much respect anybody else. If you were a merchant or a businessman or a farmer or a mechanic, you were a useful person and all that sort of thing but you did not amount to anything. To command respect all over Asia and to some extent in Europe, you had to be a soldier, or a landowner who might become a soldier at any moment, or an ecclesiastic.

Moses was a studious person with extraordinary spiritual leanings—that was what led him into that opportunity—and being the adopted son of Pharaoh's daughter, he was trained for the priesthood and he worked himself up to the highest ranks. In the New Testament we are told that Moses was learned in all the learning of the Egyptians. In those days learning was kept a profound secret for certain reasons, and as you worked up to the various ranks of the priesthood, you were told certain things. When you got halfway up, for example, you were taught geometry. Geometry was considered a valuable secret. It was used for mensuration and for putting up the pyramids and very many other things. But always remember that in the ancient world the word *geometry* also meant what we call metaphysics. What we call metaphysics was taught the students of Plato, Socrates, and Pythagoras, and it was taught by all the ancient leaders. How much they could get over to their followers was another matter. However, they put up these barriers to learning for the general public. They thought it was necessary.

But remember that the real barriers to spiritual understanding are within ourselves. There is a limit to what any one of us can learn—not a limit of time but a limit of our mentality. If we are not ready for a spiritual truth neither Moses nor Jesus Christ himself could give it to us until we are ready for it. The object of our prayers and meditations is to make ourselves ready for more understanding; and when we are ready it must come. Always it is a question of degree. The knowledge always comes when the consciousness is ready.

Now, why was Moses born in those particular circumstances at that particular time? Because they correspond to his mentality. When Moses was born as that little baby he had that mentality. He had, of course, lived before. He had studied these things, he had given his time to them, and, above all, he had tried to practice them.

The only thing you have of spiritual knowledge is what you practice. What you read in books you do not have. What you speak to others about you do not have. It is what you practice that you incorporate in the subconscious, and it is with you for the rest of this life and for future lives too. You can only take with you what you incorporate in the subconscious mind. All the rest you have to leave behind—all the things on the bookshelves and all the things you may have studied. It is what you practice that stays with you.

So Moses had practiced these things in previous lives and therefore had prepared himself for this extraordinary opportunity. Being the person he was he was naturally drawn into the succession to Abraham, to Isaac, and to Jacob. He followed on from them.

He was trained in Egypt and he worked in the temples as a student and as an Egyptian priest, and he got right up to the top ranks. There were thirty-three degrees in the

Egyptian priesthood and in the last three degrees he was taught the omnipresence of God, but the Egyptian priesthood did not teach the unreality of evil because they did not know it. It remained for Moses to get that for himself at firsthand. The Egyptian priesthood believed that with the power of good you could overcome evil, but they did believe that there was something to overcome. We believe that there is only a false belief to overcome, but they believed in actual evil to overcome.

When you study the Egyptian books you are struck by the number of different gods, and particularly the animal gods. You see gods with the head of a cat. The Egyptians were very fond of cats. I am rather fond of cats myself, but it is interesting, is it not, that the cat is the only domestic animal that does not appear in the Bible. You can go from Genesis to Revelation and you will find some surprising things, but never a cat. Well, I will leave that with you. They had gods with the head of a hawk, and gods with the heads of serpents. But the higher priesthood did not believe in those things. The upper ranks of the clergy did not think for a moment that a cat could be a god, or that a god would clothe himself in the body of a hawk or a serpent. They knew that those were *symbols*— the bull as the symbol for strength and power, the tiger and the lion as a symbol also for strength and power of another kind, the dove as a symbol for peace and diplomacy. They knew these things.

It has been the custom all through the Christian era to blame the priests of Egypt and Syria for, as they said, deceiving the people. Why did they not go to the people and tell them the truth? I suppose for several reasons. For one, they did not want the people to know too much, but after all, that failure has not been peculiar to the Egyptian priesthood. We often find people in high places today who say that it is not wise to let the people know too much, to give them too much power.

But there is another side to it. Many people do not want the higher truth, even in this twentieth century of ours. A lot of people's attitude is, "Let me alone. Leave me where I am. I am quite comfortable. Do not upset me. I don't want to go higher." The Egyptian people were exactly like us. We do not want the higher truth, any one of us, in many parts of our lives. We see the beauty of it, we love it, and we hunger for the protection that we think it has; but we keep our lives full of things with cats' heads, snakes' heads, and all kinds of things that we do not want to get rid of, rather than put the one God there instead. When you and I want to put the one God there then it will be high time to blame the Egyptians, and I think that when we reach that stage we will not want to blame them.

At any rate, there they were, and Moses was trained in that teaching. And then you know what happened. He always felt a kinship with his own people, and he went among them.

One day he saw an Egyptian beating one of his people, and here is a wonderful sidelight on the character of Moses. He immediately set upon him and beat him up. Moses was by no means perfect. He had a terrible temper in the beginning. He set upon this Egyptian and he was so angry that he beat him until he killed him. That is quite a temper—for a person high up in the priesthood. Then he buried him in the sand. Next day he was walking about again and he saw two of his own people quarreling. He stepped in. It was not his business a bit. So you see that he had something else to learn. Then one of the men said to him, "Oh, are you going to kill me as you killed that person yesterday and buried him over there?" So Moses knew that his deed was known and he cleared out of Egypt into the desert.

When he was out there he came to a well. Wells are of tremendous importance in those lands where there is very little rain. The well means life itself. It is a gathering place, a gossiping place—very much as the corner grocery store was in the old days in America, in the small towns and villages. Just where they go nowadays, I do not know—but of course now they have the party-line telephone! However, in the East, the well was the gathering place. Moses came along and he found some girls there. They were the seven daughters of a priest. Out among the Midianites we are told that the priests were mostly free lance, as we would say. They taught the people and probably did some healing, but they were not organized as in Egypt.

At any rate, this particular priest had these seven daughters who went to the well to get the water for the family for drinking purposes, and cooking and washing, and watering their flock. Some shepherds came to drive them away to get ahead of them. But Moses again could not mind his own business. So he interfered, and he seemed to be a pretty husky person. He drove off the shepherds and he helped the seven girls to get the water. And their father sent for him, and before very long—almost before Moses could turn around—he had married him off to the eldest daughter.

I want to show you that the Bible is full of real drama, real human happenings. Moses was not a statue by Michelangelo. He was a real person like you, full of difficulties, searching for God. This priest of Midian was not a statue. He was a living man with seven daughters. And as soon as a stranger came along, an eligible sort of person, a gentleman, a person of some importance—well, after all, a man with seven daughters—he married her off! All right. That is the story. They were real people, just as real as if they lived in Chicago, Los Angeles, or Brooklyn! And until we know that the people in the Bible are real people, we shall not understand the Bible and we shall not get the message.

Now consider the spiritual part of this. Always in the Bible we must ask what the name means. The Bible names always have a meaning. Moses means "drawn out of the water," and we know that "water" in the Bible stands for the human mind, the human personality, and especially the emotional nature. Of course, nine tenths of your personality is your feelings, and one tenth your knowledge. That is water, and Moses has to be drawn out of the water. It is Moses who leads the children of Israel out of Egypt.

Now we have come to an extremely important Bible symbol—Egypt. Egypt in the Bible means limitation, our belief in matter, time, space, our fear—all the things that clamp us down, the things that make us unhappy, and old, and bitter. That is Egypt. In the beginning of the Gospel of Matthew one of the things we are told about the Christ child is, "Out of Egypt have I called my son."

Egypt is always basically the same thing—a lack of faith in God. Whenever we are sick, or fearful, or depressed, what is it but a lack of faith in God? And then we are apt to say, "If God will come down and fix it up for me, I will believe in Him." What is that but a lack of faith in God right where you are? If we think, "If God will come down," we are saying really that God is not here—He is there. As soon as we begin to learn that God is with us always, that the things that seem evil are false belief, that there is substance and there is shadow, then the power of God is bringing us out of Egypt. Always the beginning of salvation is there. "Out of Egypt have I called my son."

So this child grew up and he led the people out of Egypt. Later on we shall see just how. They were in bondage in Egypt, and in order to lead them out of Egypt he had to understand what "Egypt" was. Some of the Egyptians knew. Moses knew. He had all their secrets, and in addition he knew what they did not know, what he got through secret tradition down through Abraham, Isaac, and the others.

He knew that the outer thing is only a picture. The Egyptian priesthood said, "Yes, it is real, but we can manage it." They believed in what is called mind over matter. They were very much in the position of some psychologists today. They said, "Yes, the thing is there but we can manage it. Yes, that is a tubercular lung but we can heal it." Moses, however, knew that the outer thing is only a picture and that anything that seems to be evil, no matter what it is, is still but a false belief. He knew that life is consciousness,* and only the very, very few, the very elect among the human race, have known that—until Jesus came and taught it to the people. Moses knew it. Abraham knew it. Gautama Buddha knew it. The very elect of the early Hindu teachers knew it, and although they did not keep it secret—they gave it to their students—their students could not understand it and therefore could not get it; just as Jesus tried to teach it to the Twelve Apostles and not one of them got it until after

_____

* See booklet, "Life Is Consciousness" (Unity School, Lee's Summit, Mo.).

the Day of Pentecost. They had the words but not the understanding of the thing.

Then before Moses starts his work he has to conquer himself. He has to realize that he is full of limitation. He sees himself killing someone. He sees himself interfering—a dramatization of his own faults. And so he goes into the wilderness to overcome that. The first step toward God is to realize our own unworthiness. As long as we are pleased with ourselves we cannot get to God. The most difficult barrier between men and God is self-righteousness, spiritual pride. So long as we think, "I am not such a bad person. I am pretty good. I am rather spiritual," we cannot get to God. It is not until we realize our complete unworthiness without God that we can become one with Him. Then we shall realize our worthiness but we shall know that it is within and not something separate.

So Moses had to go into the wilderness and realize his faults. That was the historical Moses, but spiritually we have to see our own faults, to see ourselves murdering Egyptians instead of realizing the Truth about them. All the time that we are fighting our problems, are we not trying to murder Egyptians? We have to stop that. And then we have to turn to God and to give some time to being with Him alone. Everyone who has ever done anything spiritually has done that. When Saul saw the light and became Paul, he went into Arabia for three years. When Jesus fully realized who he was and what he had come to do, he went into the wilderness for forty days.

Always you will find that there has to be time alone with God. If you cannot stand that, well, you will have to wait for God until you can.

So Moses goes into the wilderness. We know historically that he did meet these seven daughters, and he married one of them. That is historical, but on the spiritual side the priest stands for the approach to God.

Of course, the seven daughters are the Seven Main Aspects of God.* There are seven avenues through which humanity can approach God in the present age. There are others, but they do not concern us because they do not belong to us in the present age. There are seven different aspects of God and we learn about God by realizing these aspects. They are Life, Truth, Love, Intelligence, Soul, Spirit, Principle. Always for each of us there is one that is easier for us than the others. There is one that will be easier for us to realize and that is the one we should concentrate upon most.

Well, Moses marries one of these daughters. Always in the Bible and in Oriental literature you will find that marriage is used as the symbol for the union of God and man. The Old Testament says, "Thy Maker is thy husband," and all through the Bible the soul is spoken of as the bride, and the Christ power as the bridegroom.

And now we are told of the Israelites in Egypt, "that their cry went up to God." They were being oppressed in Egypt, but they did not sit down under it. Never sit down under your limitations. Never say, "Well, I have to put up with it." Turn to God instead and do not take "no" for an answer.

Then it says, "God heard their groaning, and God remembered His covenant . . . and took knowledge of it." You will remember that covenant in which, if we fill our minds with good and expect only good, then only good will come to us. And if we fill our minds with evil and

---

* See "The Seven Main Aspects of God" in *Alter Your Life* (Harper & Brothers), p. 119.

expect evil, evil must come to us. In proportion that evil is in our thoughts, so will trouble be in our lives. And so it says that God remembered the covenant and took mind of the children of Israel.

In Egypt the priests were also the scientists. In the modern world there has been a quarrel between religion and science, or I should say there has been a quarrel between the churches and science. There can be no quarrel between true religion and science, but there has been a quarrel between the Christian churches and science going back about four hundred years. This, I suppose, reached its culmination in the victory of science in the Victorian age, in the days of Huxley, Tyndall, and the others.

But in Egypt in the time of Moses there was no such quarrel. The priests were learned men. They knew a great deal about astronomy. If you examine the writings on the Great Pyramid, you will be amazed at the knowledge of astronomy that the builders had. (I know that the Pyramid was not built by true Egyptians, but they took part in it under the direction of others.) They had a great deal of knowledge of the human mind—of psychology. They had a great deal of what we call today "occult" knowledge. They knew a great deal about the ether and how to manipulate it, and they had a great knowledge of agriculture and other subjects, much of which was afterward lost. The better educated Egyptian could have taught the best educated Greeks a thing or two. He could have taught the Romans something, and he could have taught the Europeans in the Dark Ages a great deal.

Moses, as we have seen, was brought up in that. He learned all about these things, and he learned things that no college or textbook could teach—things that only God teaches direct. And, of course, he also learned by experience. As a rule, the great drawback to academic people is that they know nothing about life. The trouble with our professors is that, like the Lady of Shalott, they turn their backs on the world and look into a mirror, the mirror being a book, and they see men not as they are, but as they are reflected in books and libraries.

For instance, most people in Europe think that Woodrow Wilson was a great man. I do not wish to touch upon a controversial subject, because in America we are still too near him to judge him. He cannot really be judged for some generations yet. However, in Europe they think he was a very great man and a very disinterested man, but they believe his career was spoiled by lack of knowledge of life. He knew everything that could be found in a book, everything that the head of a great university—Princeton—could possibly know, but *he knew nothing of real life.* That is the general opinion in Europe. He did not know men and women as they are, but as they are written of in books. So when he went to Europe and found those extremely sophisticated people, Lloyd George, Clemenceau, and Orlando, who did not know much of what was in books, so far as one could discover, but who knew everything outside them, Mr. Wilson got very much the worst of it. I mention that in passing because human nature remains very much the same. Although conditions of life in the Old World were different from those of today, human nature was much the same. It takes thousands of years for human nature to change very much.

Moses, however, went among the general public, the common people, and learned to understand them; consequently, he balanced his academic knowledge with a practical knowledge of life. He knew people and he knew human nature. He loved mankind, but as he looked around him he was saddened at the unnecessary suffering in the world. He saw all kinds of men and women, from the king of Egypt whom he knew and the people in the court, down to the laboring brickmakers whom he also knew. He saw them suffering unnecessarily, worrying, wearing themselves out, living a difficult and uncertain life, and dying prematurely—very much as we see about us today.

So he decided he would put his knowledge at their disposal. He knew the causes of their suffering and unhappiness. He knew why they were wasting their lives and not getting anywhere—because they spent their time struggling with the outer thing, and leaving their consciousness unchanged. He knew that as long as people did that, even if they did it for a million years, the world would still be full of strife, wars, labor troubles, booms followed by depressions, and so forth. So he set to work and drew up his teaching in a manner that he thought best calculated to help everybody.

First of all, he wanted to help the people who did not think—who accepted everything at its face value—but who needed some rough and ready rules to go by. So he put his rules in the form of Commandments in order that they would be understood by that kind of people.

But he knew that there is a stage beyond this and that when people reached that stage they needed something more.

Moses, who was one of the greatest prophets who ever lived, got his knowledge of the human heart. Then when he had prayed and meditated, he received his inspiration direct from God—he got his illumination. He set down and described the human soul and the way it works. He described it in this writing, which we break into ten clauses and call the Ten Commandments.

In the Bible they are very brief, very concise, whereas our modern psychology is extremely nebulous and windy and wordy. If you ever try to read Freud, you will see at once what I mean. You know how Freud takes ten pages to say what a newspaperman might say in five, what a good writer might say in three, and what Moses said in one. In that one page there is more about the working of the human mind than in all the writings of the modern psychologists, to say nothing of the ancient ones.

The Ten Commandments at their face value are true and valid, but that is only the beginning. If people are going to get anywhere, if they are going to escape from the continuous strife and struggle of life, they must have something more.

So within these Commandments he concealed the laws of psychology for those who were ready for them. And within that again, he concealed the deepest and highest spiritual teaching for those who were ready for that.

In other words, Moses designed these laws of life so that the higher we go spiritually, or the deeper we go intellectually, the more we can get out of them.

CHAPTER 2

By Right of Consciousness

Thou shalt not steal.

EXODUS 20:15

*And the people stood afar off, and Moses drew near unto
the thick darkness where God was.*

EXODUS 20:21

S CIENTIFIC prayer is the most important thing
in the world, and so I am going to begin right
down at the fifteenth verse of Exodus 20, "Thou
shalt not steal," because that Commandment really gives
us the clue to scientific prayer. If you like to call it the
Eighth Commandment, well and good. It does not matter in what order you put them. One does not have to
take the Ten Commandments chronologically because
actually they are not quite in a logical order.

However, let us consider the true meaning of this Commandment, one of the fundamental laws of life, revealed
to Moses in this particular form. Others had these laws
before Moses. They were known in ancient India, and

before that. But these laws of life and human psychology
came to Moses in this clear way and he put them down. So
that is the form in which we of the Western world have received them, and I think it is the clearest and best form.

"Thou shalt not steal." Many people will say, "Well,
what then? We always knew that we must not steal. If we
do we shall have difficulty and trouble and probably wind
up in prison." Now, I know that churchgoing people, and
the people who read religious books, do not usually pick
pockets, or blow safes, or take money out of a drawer, or
steal an automobile, but I want us to realize that that is
only the outside surface meaning of it.

All through the ages it is only the smallest percentage
of human beings who have ever stolen anything. Respect
for other people's property is a primitive instinct. So
Moses did not take the trouble of writing down these
laws of life just to tell people they were not to steal. He
wrote them down because he wanted to teach his people to go far beyond the outer, right into the very heart
of human conduct—because "Thou shalt not steal" really means "Thou *canst* not steal."

These laws of life, these Ten Commandments, are not,
in their essence, merely prohibitions like "No smoking,"
or "No left turn," or "No exit."

Moses did not take the trouble just to tell people they
must not steal. These Ten Commandments really mean
"Thou *canst* not do these things." For example, I can say
to you—it would sound eccentric—"Thou shalt not swim
the Atlantic Ocean," and I know perfectly well that as
long as you live, even if you live to be as old as Methuse-
lah, you will never swim the Atlantic. I know that. But I am
not really saying that you must not, but that you won't—
no matter how long you live on this earth plane. You may,
if you reach a sufficiently high degree of understanding,

translate yourself across the Atlantic, as Jesus translated himself across the lake, but you will never *swim* the Atlantic. So when I say, "Thou shalt not swim the Atlantic," I am not forbidding you to swim the Atlantic. I am saying that you won't swim the Atlantic because you cannot.

In these ten laws of life, when Moses says, "Thou shalt not," he means "You cannot." This most fundamental law of life means that we cannot steal.

You may say, "I know several people who have done so." No, you may know someone who broke into your house and took your silver. You may know that when you hung up your coat in a restaurant someone took your wallet out of the pocket. But did they steal? They tried, but did they succeed? No, the man who took ten dollars out of your pocket will not get away with it. The burglar who took your silver actually transferred some silver from your house to someone else's house, but did he get away with it? He did not. If that silver belonged to you by right of consciousness, all the burglars in the world could not have taken it away, and if you had the understanding of the presence of God in all men, no one could have taken your wallet. In fact, if you had this understanding, you could take a thousand dollar bill—perhaps I had better say a ten dollar bill because many people, if they saw a thousand dollar bill, would be like the old lady who saw a giraffe for the first time, and said, "I don't believe it. There ain't no such animal"—you could take a ten dollar bill, put it on the sidewalk in Times Square, and return the next day and it would still be there. Your consciousness of the presence of God in other people would have been so strong that no one could have taken from you what belonged to you by right of that consciousness.

Some people talk as though you could do anything you want to, while others seem to think that you are a puppet of destiny with no choice at all. They are both wrong. The truth is that you can do anything, have anything, be anything, for which you have the consciousness—but not otherwise.

To be healthy, you must have a health consciousness. To be prosperous, you must have a prosperity consciousness. To be successful in any field of endeavor, you must have the consciousness that corresponds. There is a slang expression that says that to accomplish anything difficult "you must have what it takes." Well, what it "takes" is the consciousness to correspond with it.

To try to get something without having the consciousness to which it belongs is really mental theft. That, of course, cannot succeed—"Thou shalt not steal," which really means "Thou canst not steal."

So when Moses says, "Thou shalt not," he means "Thou canst not."

These ten laws of life are things that cannot be done, and so, says the great prophet in effect, do not waste yourself or your life trying to do these things. They cannot be done. They conflict with the fundamental Law of Being.

We cannot steal. History is full, unfortunately, of examples of where it was attempted and sometimes looked very successful for the time being, but the mills of God grind slowly and the thing cannot work because it is a breach of the law. We cannot keep anything for which we do not have the consciousness to correspond.

We cannot steal, and the sooner we realize that fact the sooner we shall give up trying. When we give up trying to steal, then we shall begin to have our own. We shall come into our own rights, our own property—using the word *property* in the widest sense of the conditions that belong to us—and when we get that, liberation will not be very far off.

Moses, of course, was a practical man. All the great teachers are practical. Anyone who understands his subject can always explain it in simple words. Moses used the simplest words: he knew his subject. Jesus used the simplest words: he knew his subject. Teachers and writers who are vague and nebulous are so because they do not understand their subject. Moses was clear and practical and he did a practical job. Each one must live a practical life. You have your business to go to, your home to manage, your practice to take care of, whatever it may be. If you are to make any spiritual progress you must be doing something of use in the world, and demonstrating there. If you retire to the wilderness, as the saints and anchorites did, you cease to develop. Jesus said not to do that but to stay *in* the world and demonstrate there. All those who make spiritual progress are doing something useful in the world and demonstrating there.

Well, Moses had his practical job to do. His people were in bondage to a foreign power. That has constantly happened in the history of the world, just as it is happening, for example, to the Czechs and the Poles, for the time being. Moses' people were in bondage to a foreign and powerful nation, and it was the job of Moses to get them away; just as it was the job of Garibaldi two centuries ago to set Italy free from the Austrian rule, and just as it was the historical job of George Washington to get the United States their freedom. So it was the job of Moses to get his people out of their conditions and start them off in a new way of life, build up a new psychology, a new ethic, and a new approach to God.

It was quite a job. Moses did not want to undertake it in the first place, but when it was all over, he was glad. He did not find his people easy to handle. I heard Rabbi Wise say at a Carnegie Hall meeting, that after having been leader of his congregation for a number of years, he could fully appreciate the difficulties that Moses had faced centuries before!

For example, Egypt had been very comfortable. Although it is true that they were in slavery, in many respects it was a comfortable slavery. They did not particularly want a new way of life. However, he got them on the march, men, women, and children. He got the people out and across the Red Sea—you all know the story—and into the wilderness.

The same thing has been done in modern times. That was the work the Mormon people did in Utah, but on a much smaller scale, in different surroundings. Brigham Young was perhaps the greatest of our Western pioneers. Now please do not think that I approve of Brigham Young's views on marriage. I do not. I hope that no one will take it upon himself to say, "Dr. Fox is approving of Brigham Young's family arrangements." I do not. I think he would have been a much greater man without polygamy, but I think that, despite that fact, he did a great work.

He took his people across the wilderness that the prairies were at that time, surrounded by hostile savages, took them into the desert, as Utah was then, and they have turned that desert very largely into a garden. They would have done that even better, of course, without polygamy. Incidentally, we are told that Brigham Young did not approve of polygamy himself. It is said that when Joseph Smith told him he must have at least a dozen wives, he went sadly home, and passing a funeral on the way, he envied the corpse.

At any rate, Moses had his practical job. He had these people, of all sorts and types, many of them primitive and ignorant, many of them highly cultured in the Egyptian tradition, and he had to get them out of that civilized country. He had to be ruthless. They had to march along in companies and behave themselves for the general good. He had to organize a police force, and he did. The people had to be fed, the camps kept sanitary, and so forth. These things are easy to do in an army where there is discipline. In an army there are men, but here there were men, women, and children, and discipline was a very difficult thing. So Moses couched his laws of life in such plain language that the simplest, most ignorant material person would get something out of it—the kind of person who would steal somebody's shoes, or somebody's bed. And yet the people who were prepared for something higher could also get it from these Commandments. So these Ten Commandments function on every level. When people are so simple, so primitive that they will steal, they are told not to. Those who are a little above that are ready for something higher.

Now, there is one great fundamental law, the Law of Being, the summing up of all laws in life, and it is this: whatever comes to you, whatever happens to you, whatever surrounds you, will be in accordance with your consciousness, and nothing else; that whatever is in your consciousness must happen, no matter who tries to stop it; and whatever is not in your consciousness cannot happen. People do not know that, but it means, in other words, "Thou canst not steal."

Now what is stealing? What is theft, or as the law likes to call it, larceny? What is stealing? Stealing is trying to get something for which we do not have the consciousness, and are therefore not spiritually entitled to. That is stealing. Oh, you may be the most respectable person, complete with top hat, who ever walked down Fifth Avenue on an Easter Sunday. You may be the most respectable person in the parish, so much so that you would not dream of stealing a thing. But you may be trying to steal credit that does not belong to you. You may be pretending to be very learned without learning. You may be pretending to be very rich when you are nearly broke. Then there are other people who do not care about money, but they are snobs. They think it very fine to talk about "my cousin, Lord Somebody." They think a person with a high position in the world is better than a person with a lower position. They would like to be high up in the world, so they pretend to have some social importance that they do not have. It is easier to do that in Europe than in America, but it can be done. Even in America there are a few snobs, not many, but there are a few. In England, what is easier, for example, than to refer to your cousin, Lord So-and-So?

There are others who do not care about social life, but they want to pretend that they have done something good. So they say they have done it. They boast and they brag, and boasting and bragging is a form of theft. Most of us have met the old fellow who says he knocked out John L. Sullivan, when he probably never saw John L. And we have met the other fellow who swam the Channel, and who really never went more than a hundred yards from shore. But he wants us to think he was a successful athlete. And so on and on and on.

Whenever we are trying to get credit that we are not entitled to, we are trying to steal. The fact that we may not deceive other people in the long run does not matter. What does matter is that we are damaging our own soul.

Most of us would not want to do these stupid or cheap things, but we can try to steal in other ways. We can try to steal by fooling ourselves. For example, if we are not demonstrating, and we say to ourselves, "I have not had any demonstrations for quite a time. There is something wrong and I must find out what it is," that is fine. However, if we say, "I am not demonstrating in the outer but in ways that you cannot see," or, "I cannot demonstrate that right now, but at the right time, it will come," we are fooling ourselves, and we are trying to steal. We are trying to enjoy a spiritual success that we do not have the consciousness for. Even if we are trying to deceive nobody but ourself—often that is the fellow we are trying to deceive—we cannot do it. We cannot keep anything for which we do not have the consciousness.

Now, with will power you can snatch something for perhaps a short time, but you cannot keep it. That is what gambling is. Did it ever strike you what gambling really is? It is not throwing money on a green cloth and watching the wheel roll around. It is trying to get something for which you do not have the consciousness. Everybody should go to Monte Carlo at least once. No show in Europe for which you pay admission is half as interesting. What is gambling? It is trying to get something to which you are not entitled by right of consciousness. It may be roulette, the hospital sweepstakes, backing horses, but it is trying to get some money to which you are not entitled by consciousness. "Thou canst not steal."

So the great Law of Life is that you cannot keep anything for which you do not have the consciousness. If you have the consciousness, you would not have to try to steal it. On the other hand, you cannot lose anything for which you have the consciousness. When we merely try to get things in the outer, we are wasting our time and our lives.

Moses knew that. He was a cultured man. He had received the very highest education that Egypt could give. He rose in the priesthood to the very top rank—as I have mentioned, there were thirty-three rungs of the ladder—and he knew all that teaching. He was a great occultist, but he knew that occultism is not God, and that he was the master of it and not the servant. He saw around him all kinds of people, from the simplest up to the king, wasting their lives trying to change things in the outer, just as we do right here in New York today, trying to change our lives and change things by tampering with the outer picture.

So he wrote these laws of life. He said that you cannot do or have anything without the consciousness for it. As you get the consciousness, no one can keep your good from you. So do not bother with the outer picture but change your consciousness.

You cannot do anything that is not in accordance with your consciousness at the moment, but you can change your consciousness. No one can stop you. You can go to work and change your consciousness now through scientific prayer. Is not that the real object of the metaphysical teaching—the Jesus Christ teaching? I think it is. So as soon as we know that we can change our consciousness through scientific prayer, then we have the key to life.

Now, scientific prayer or spiritual treatment is really the lifting or changing of your consciousness by withdrawing your attention from the outer picture for the time being and then concentrating gently upon spiritual Truth. You may do this by reading the Bible or any spiritual book that appeals to you, by going over any hymn or poem that helps you in this way, or by the use of affirmations, just as you like. When you use affirmations you must affirm the Presence of God with you, and then claim that He is bringing into your life the particular good which you desire.

That is building the new consciousness and that means that you are also building a new life.

CHAPTER 3

Thoughts Are Things

*Thou shalt not take the name of the Lord thy God in vain;
for the Lord will not hold him guiltless that taketh his
name in vain.*

EXODUS 20:7

N OW this Commandment, this law of life, goes
a step further. "Thou shalt not take the name
of the Lord thy God in vain; for the Lord will
not hold him guiltless that taketh his name in vain." You
know now, of course, that that really means you *cannot*
take the name of the Lord *in vain*. If you try to do so you
will fail because when you take the name of God unto
yourself and implement it, then the consequences must
and will follow.

It is a pity more of us do not realize that because constantly we are trying to take the name of the Lord in vain.
That does not simply mean mentioning the name of God.
Many people do use the name of God very lightly, but
this Commandment or law of life means a great deal
more than that because the name of God is not simply its

sound, but the name of God is your conviction concerning God.

What do you think of the nature of God? What do you think God is like? That is the most important question in the whole world because your idea of God will determine your whole life. From the very marrow of your bones right down to the farthest place your influence goes, all is determined ultimately by your real belief about the nature of God.

You may say, "Oh, that's easy. I learned my church catechism and I can repeat it." That absolutely does not mean a thing. You may know the shorter catechism or the Thirty-nine Articles by heart, and irrespective of whether they are true or false, it does not mean a thing. What matters is your real belief about God. If you say, "The truth is that it's so hazy I don't know what I think about God"—and that is true of many people—then it will leave your life hazy, drifting, and undetermined. It is your conception of the nature of God that makes your whole life. It makes you what you are. It makes your health, your appearance, your home, your business. It makes the kinds of friends and enemies you have and the kind of people you meet. Of all the important things that should be taken care of, the one thing that really matters is your idea of God, because that determines everything. You cannot have that in vain.

Your idea of God is not the name you give to God. It does not matter what you call God. We say God; the Germans say Gott; the French say Le Bon Dieu, and so forth. In Sanskrit it is Diva, The Shining One. These are only names. The real name of God for you is *your idea* of God; not mine, not the one your father or mother taught you, not the local minister's idea, but your own honest and real idea of God. That will govern your whole life. That is the name of God for you, and you cannot have it in vain.

That is what the Bible means when it says, "Thou shalt not take the name of the Lord thy God in vain." You cannot do it. If your idea of God is a lofty one, approximate to the Truth, things will go well with you. If your idea of God is a false one, a long way from the Truth, things will go ill with you. It is true of you; it is true of nations; it is true of churches; it is true of races. All is determined by your idea of the nature of God.

The question is sometimes asked, "Do you believe in God?" But that question and its answer can have no meaning until you say what kind of God you believe in. Then it has a meaning.

There is no one who does not believe in something. The so-called atheist or materialist always believes in the laws of nature. I suppose the most militant atheists of the present day are the Marxists, the self-styled followers of Marx—although Marx would probably excommunicate them if he could come back. They have an anti-God department in the Russian Government, or used to. Yet they all believe most pathetically in the laws of nature. So they are simply calling God nature, that is all. All these materialists believe in the laws of chemistry and physics. They believe in engineering. They say the brain secretes thought as the liver secretes bile, and that the laws of nature are unchanging, and so forth. They believe in the laws of nature and that is their idea of God.

There are people in parts of Africa, for instance, who get a cocoanut and put a couple of beads in it and call it a god. They believe in that, and that is their idea of God.

I have met orthodox people who believed really that God was an old gentleman living up in the clouds, very much like the bishop they once met, but living up in the

sky. That was their idea of God. There are more thoughtful people of the same type who think of God as a com-
mittee of three men, and that is their idea of God.

So you see the only intelligent question is what kind
of God do you believe in, because everybody believes in
some God, even those who do not like the word. And
you cannot believe in any kind of God without getting
the result of that. If you say that you do not know what
God is like, you get the result of that, with any amount of
confusion and drifting.

Now, whatever idea of God you really have, that is the
name of God for you, and it cannot fail to have its effect.
You cannot take the name of the Lord in vain, for the
Lord will not hold him guiltless who taketh His name in
vain.

In the Bible idiom God is often represented as speaking like a man, just as in some of the old-fashioned children's stories, when a child had gotten his clothing wet,
the wind and the sun are represented as speaking to the
child and saying, "We'll dry it for you."

So Moses says that you cannot escape from the result of
your idea of God, and whatever your idea of God is, will
affect your life in every way. There is no getting away from
that. "The Lord will not hold him guiltless that taketh his
name in vain." If you believe that God is good, God is
love, God has all power, God is intelligence, all the conditions of your life will steadily improve. Some difficulties will clear up much sooner than others. Some people
will demonstrate harmony and well-being sooner than
others. These things are only a matter of degree. But
when you really believe that God is all these things, as
unquestioningly, as unemotionally as you believe in the
soundness of the George Washington Bridge when you
cross it in a car, then everything will begin to come right.

Details may challenge you. You may get a pain somewhere, just as though the "lower self" were saying, "What about this?" If you still believe in the oneness and goodness and power of God, you will overcome it. Then something distressing comes along in business, just as though an inanimate thing could challenge you, saying, "Here is that contract gone wrong again," or, "That other firm has gone broke so that you can't get your money." But you hold on to the Truth of Being, and that difficulty comes right. Then probably someone of whom you had a high opinion disappoints you because he turns out to be silly or weak. It is just as though again an impersonal law said, "What about this now?" You still hold on to the Truth. As you hold on, through test after test to what you know to be the Truth—because you know that you cannot take the name of God in vain—then the name of God cannot be without power for you.

If you really believe there is no God at all except the laws of nature, you are under that dominion, and limited in every possible way. You have no way of rising above the laws of nature because you believe in them. Those materialists who believe in these laws cannot rise above them. They are under their dominion.

If you believe God is intelligent but not good—I know people would not dare to say that, but people who think that God sends sickness and trouble really believe in a God Who is not good—if you believe in a God Who has all intelligence, all power, but a God Who is not loving, Who is not good, then that is your idea of the nature of God, and it cannot be in vain for you. It must work out. All kinds of difficulties and troubles will come to you, and you will not overcome them because you are saying, "God sent this trouble for a good purpose, and I must put up with it." All right. You *will* put up with it. You will not overcome it. Your idea of God cannot be in vain. It must work out for you in accordance with your belief, not your nominal or formal belief, but your real one.

There are plenty of us who in practice believe that God can do certain things but not others. We would not admit that. It would sound silly, but in practice we often believe it. I have told you the story of the man who had a lawsuit against him in London. A decision was given against him that seemed to mean ruin. He came to me full of woe, and I said, "We are going to hold right on to the Truth of Being. We know that God can bring this thing right, and to the satisfaction of all concerned." Within a very few weeks the whole thing did come right. For the time being, he had been inclined to say that God could do anything except get him justice over the lawsuit, that He could not do that because the High Court had decided against it. The thing was through with. What could God do?

Other people believe that God can prosper their business but cannot give them health because they are having difficulty in demonstrating health. Other people always have buoyant health, and if they get a cold or anything, in five minutes, it seems, it is gone. They believe that God can do anything with health, and they are impatient of sick people because they are so well themselves. But they cannot make a go of it in business, and they think that somehow God cannot do anything about that.

We need to watch ourselves. I do not think there is any one of us who is not limiting God in some respect in his thought, and because of that we are going to suffer limitation in some way, for we cannot take the name of God in vain.

You take the name of God by your idea of God. In the early days many people took a superficial view of this.

They thought that the actual name of God must not be spoken, and among the Hebrews one of the names of God was not allowed to be uttered. That was a superstition because merely mentioning a name has no meaning one way or the other. It is the thought that counts. They did not understand that the thing that was important was not the question of mentioning the name of God but that they must not have a limited idea of God. Hence the Bible tells us that people get into difficulties because they limit the Holy One of Israel.

So Moses says here, you cannot take the name of the Lord thy God in vain. You *cannot* do it. Whatever your idea of God is, whatever idea you really believe in, that is what will be expressed in your life. A limited God will be limited, a cruel God will react on you cruelly and without love. You will suffer the results of that. If you believe in a weak God, you will suffer the consequences of weakness. If you believe in a human God, you will have all the trouble you would have if a human being really could run this universe. And if you look around this little earth planet and see what a job man has made of it up to date, I think you will find no further comment necessary.

However, if you believe that God is spirit, and think what spirit means, and if you believe God is love, and intelligence and life, and wisdom, and think what these things mean, and *really believe* it, you will get the result of that kind of God. Your conditions will improve as the days and weeks go by. You will go from strength to strength. Your health, your surroundings, and your understanding will increase and multiply—until "the daybreak and the shadows flee away" altogether—because you cannot take the name of God in vain.

CHAPTER 4

I Am That I Am

*I am the Lord thy God, which have brought thee out of the
land of Egypt, out of the house of bondage.
Thou shalt have no other gods before me.*

EXODUS 20:2, 3

IN our study of the Ten Commandments, which
are, as we know, really an expression of the laws
of mind, we have gotten to the place where we
are handling what is often called the First Commandment. It was necessary that we should come to it in this way,
and not chronologically, in order to get a more intelligent idea of what the Commandments stand for.

We have seen that the Commandments, at their face
value, are perfectly true and valid. Their simple, superficial meaning is a good one.

But, of course, we are going to go much deeper than
this. The whole of this extraordinary document is a study
in the way in which man's mind works.

The account begins with these thunderings and lightnings on the mount, and the fear of the people that they

39

must not go up the mount unless they are thoroughly prepared, and so forth. But the Bible always means Me— I who read it. I have often said that in principle I wish that every Bible had printed on the cover, "This means ME," because everything in the Bible is a study in human psychology and metaphysics. It is only secondarily a historical book. Many of the things in the Bible never really happened. They are not actual fact but they are instruction in psychology and metaphysics; and in order that they would have a message for people in various stages of spiritual development throughout the ages, they are written in parable and symbol.

Jesus said, for example, "A certain man went down from Jerusalem to Jericho." A parable. There never was that particular man. He says, "A certain man owned a vineyard." There never was such a man. There was never such a man as Adam, nor such a woman as Eve.* They never existed. That is another parable. The Bible is primarily and almost entirely a study in psychology, and so everybody in the Bible is every man.

Moses, however, did exist just as surely as there was a Napoleon and a George Washington. He did live in Egypt over three thousand years ago, and he did take that particular nation, some six hundred thousand people, out of Egypt and into the wilderness. That is historical.

There is another historical fact that I think is interesting. Moses was a priest of the Temple of the King of Heliopolis. A temple was a university in those days. The ruins of the temple are still there and can be seen. Outside the temple of Heliopolis in the time of Moses there were four great obelisks, representing the four parts of man— like the four horses of the Apocalypse—and they are still

---

* See "Adam and Eve" in *Alter Your Life*, p. 62.

in existence. And one of them is right here in New York in Central Park. It is called Cleopatra's Needle, but, of course, it has no more to do with Cleopatra than it has with the man in the moon. It was originally there in Heliopolis and it is interesting as we walk or drive through Central Park to remember that Moses often looked at it as he went out of the temple. There are three others, and they are still in existence. One is in Paris in that great square, the Place de la Concorde, one is in Constantinople, and one is in London on the Thames embankment. In the last war the pedestal was chipped but the obelisk was not touched. It is still going strong, even as the Ten Commandments, and I think it is rather interesting that that should be so.

Well now, Moses also stands for a faculty in yourself, and the things that Moses did typify your states of mind. The Bible always is concerned with states of mind; and history and parable are used simply as illustrations of that.

Now, the mountain always means prayer or treatment—the elevated consciousness. We are told that the general public were not allowed to go up Mount Sinai, but that does not mean that certain people were not good enough to go up, because the whole thing applies to each one of us individually. It means that if we want to go up the mountain—if we want to raise our consciousness, if we want to get closer to God—we must prepare ourselves by prayer. If we try to force our way up we shall get hurt. We can usually force something for a time by willpower. However, willpower is the counterfeit of God-power, and when we use willpower to force our way up the mountain, and bring our meanness, and our self-pity, and our hatred with us, in the end we shall only get into greater difficulties.

We are told that the high priest could go up. That does not mean a certain privileged man. It does not mean that any particular clergyman, priest, minister, bishop, or moderator, or any Truth teacher or practitioner, or anyone else, has any more influence with God than you have. If you think that then you are making an idol. That is exactly why the ground for the First Commandment, "I am the Lord thy God; thou shalt have no other gods before me," is prepared by this treatise on Mount Sinai.

It is as old as the hills, this belief that someone else has more power with God than we have. We are very prone to think that because, first, most of us are lazy—at least mentally—and it is nice to think that some other fellow can do it for us; and second, because, human nature being what it is, there are always some people who pretend to have more power. They like to think that they are important, and that makes them feel important. From the very oldest religion down to the newest, there have been these people because human nature remains very much the same. It takes thousands and thousands of years for it to change. Even in the metaphysical movement I have met men and women who set themselves up as healers and teachers, and said to the public, in effect, "I know lots of things that you don't. I am very near God, and you will have to work through me." They were just copying the oldest priesthoods. They did it in the oldest priesthoods in Egypt—and in Atlantis long before Egypt—making the old, old, old mistake.

The truth is that we are as near to God as our consciousness will bring us, and no outside arrangement will do that. People who are really near to God are the very last ones who will talk about it, let alone boast of it.

If we want to go up the mountain, we have to become a high priest spiritually and not in external ways, and we must leave the common things outside. Now, remember, when I read the Bible, I am everybody in it. So are you.

Your soul is the whole of this host of people. The so-called "common people" in the text applies to all of our faults and weaknesses—these are the common people. They must stay away—we must rid ourselves of our faults and weaknesses—or we cannot go up the mountain, we cannot elevate our consciousness and get our contact with God.

If you try to get your contact with God when you are full of cruelty, jealousy, self-pity, and so forth, you will not succeed. That is why Jesus, when he taught the same thing from a different angle hundreds of years later, said, "Before you go up to the temple to pray, you must forgive your brother and make yourself right with everyone." You will remember that he said that in the Sermon on the Mount, and reiterated it in the Lord's Prayer. He tells of the publican and the sinner, and says, "If you are going up to the temple at Jerusalem, and you remember you have something against your brother, or he against you, put your gift down, fix that thing first, and then make your gift to the temple."

So Moses says here, in the same way, that the common people cannot go up Mount Sinai—that is, our lower selves, and our lower thoughts and feelings.

Now, "it came to pass that there were thunders and lightnings, and a thick cloud," and so forth. These are dramatic expressions of the change of consciousness as we move away from the common things of life to the higher things. Actually, there probably were thunder and lightning and a thick cloud upon the mountain, because man's mind has full dominion over nature, and what man believes happens.

I am going to startle some of you now. I am going to tell you that what we call nature and climate and weather is really the outpicturing of the thoughts and feelings of humanity upon it. As time goes on the human mind changes; so will the climate, the weather, and the conditions of the globe change too. I said just now that it takes thousands of years to change human nature. I meant, of course, without prayer or treatment. That is the gradual evolution of the race. The reason the North Pole is cold and the equator is warm is that the whole of humanity thinks that way. Of course, lots of people have never heard of the Pole, but the race thought thinks that. In London years ago, and when I first came to America, over at the Biltmore Hotel, I said that there was a time when the poles were warm and tropical, and that such a time would come again. Of course, I was pooh-poohed. I had one letter written by a young gentleman, more in sorrow than in anger, who gave me a lesson in physical geography and said he was very sorry to hear a public man talk that way, and hoped I would not do it again, that he was telling me for my own good, and so on. However, since then a very distinguished scientist spoke on the radio, and said that he had been giving evidence before Congress. Congress was called on to vote money for the Byrd Expedition. This man who was a geologist testified that there is a great deal of coal at the South Pole, and the reason it was there was because, hundreds of thousands of years ago, the poles were tropical. And Congress accepted the testimony without demur, and voted the money.

Now in these days of the Exodus, and around that time, the conditions of the outer world answered very quickly to man's thoughts because people believed it. That is why Moses was able to walk dry shod across the Red Sea, because he really did that. He was able to demonstrate a dry passage across the Red Sea through the power of prayer. Some modern divines cannot quite swallow that.

They have so little faith in God, and so little faith in the power of prayer, that they feel it cannot be true. They think that if anyone could walk across the Hudson River, for example, they themselves could, but because they cannot, they think that Moses could not cross the Red Sea dry shod.

But Moses took his people across the Red Sea by the power of thought, and he was able to do that because in those days people believed in the power of thought. They really did believe that mountains could be moved by faith. They believed that God could take them across the Red Sea dry shod, and He did. Today we do not believe it. We are just emerging from the Victorian age, the age of materialism and hypocrisy. In that age people believed in the fixed laws of nature, and they did not believe we had power in our thought.

Now the world is changing. Today everybody is beginning to believe in the power of thought. Psychology is as popular today (much of it not very good psychology either), and as highly thought of, as physics and chemistry were sixty or seventy years ago.

So quite likely the mountain did smoke, because the people believed it could. Well, Moses went up in the mountain, got away from the people, and established his contact with God. He had been preparing for that for many years. He had, as we have seen, a great deal of knowledge of the material world, which he got as an Egyptian priest. He also had the true knowledge of God from his father's people, the Hebrews. It was the historical mission of the Hebrews to teach that God is not a limited, corporeal being, but incorporeal, infinite, divine mind. He had worked these things out for himself too, but he had many faults and difficulties to overcome. That is why the career of Moses is so very encouraging for us—because he did not start out perfect. He started out full of faults, as we do, and he overcame them. He got his self-control. Then, by realizing the presence of God, by treatment as we call it—the Golden Key,* if you like—he got away from the limited picture. In Egypt every street corner had a shrine with gods, some of them very horrible, most of them with the heads of animals, and so forth. He got away from all that, and realized the presence of God to such an extent that he rose to a very great height, and saw clearly the laws of thought. He saw clearly the unity of God and man, and the unity of man and man. He got more than a flash of what we call the cosmic consciousness. That was his illumination. Then he realized that he must give this to humanity. He thought it out very carefully. His first instinct would be to try to give it through the Egyptian people because they were highly civilized. They had great material power and resources, and were extremely intelligent in an intellectual, materialistic way. So he thought of putting it out through them, but he realized that they were too wedded to their comforts and their civilization and their own ways of living. They were too conventional. Jesus found the same thing years later when he tried to give his message through the official people.

Then Moses decided he would have to put it out through the Hebrews, and it was hopeless to do it while they were in Egypt. Most of them were persecuted, kept down, illiterate, laboring people; and those who were not, were getting on so well that they just could not be got to drop that and take the message. He realized that the only way was to get them out of Egypt into the wilderness, away from the fleshpots, away from temptation,

---

* See *Power Through Constructive Thinking*, p. 137.

away from the conditions of being fashionable and correct, financially secure, and all the rest of it—the guise in which the "devil" sometimes comes to people. Moses realized he must get them away from that, out into the wilderness. He knew that they would not like it. He knew that he could get them away but he also knew that as soon as they were out there they would presently wish themselves back. So he had to get them right across the Red Sea where they could not get back. Then he decided to keep them there for a full generation so that the people who would start the new work would be the ones born in the desert and brought up there. The old life with all its meretricious attractions would be dead, and the older people, who knew and remembered Egypt, would have passed on. The people he would really work with would have been born in the desert and brought up in an atmosphere of spiritual expression, not one of materialism. They would have been brought up in the desert where they would have a good many physical hardships, and in an atmosphere of having to put God first.

And we know that he did that. He got them right out there. They were in the wilderness, as the Bible says, for forty years. Forty years is nearly two generations. Statisticians usually reckon a generation as twenty-five years, or thirty years if we want to be very conservative. However, among that Oriental people who mature early, where most women are married by sixteen, forty years would be two generations; not literally forty years, but thereabouts. Forty years, in the Bible, means a long span, a long time.

So Moses had his revelation, and then he realized it as experience that God and man are one. We all have it as knowledge, but it has to come as experience. He knew as experience that God and man are one, and that man and man are one. When he got that revelation, he afterward expressed but the remnant of it because, with a wonderful spiritual experience, it is impossible to bring it all back. When the contact fades out, as it were, only a few drops can be brought back. However, he brought enough back to give the laws of life, and the nature of God. So he started off by giving the First Commandment, as we call it.

What is the beginning of the First Commandment? We all think we know but do we realize it? It begins by saying, "I am"—your identity. "I am the Lord thy God." That is the beginning. The beginning of the whole Bible, the first four words in Genesis, are, "In the beginning God." Our trouble in our religious life nearly always is that we usually think, "In the beginning Me." That is very human but it does not get us the revelation that Moses got. "In the beginning Me" keeps us right where we are. I suppose that nineteen times out of twenty, when prayers fail and spiritual life seems to peter out, the real reason is that we are working on the basis of "In the beginning Me," whereas the Bible says, "In the beginning God."

So the First Commandment says, "I am the Lord thy God; thou shalt have no other gods before me." To have other gods is idolatry, and that is the blanket sin. It is the term that covers all evil. Every kind of sin that man can commit boils down to idolatry because he is putting something before God. There is only one God Who is the only presence and the only power.

Genesis says, "In the beginning God," and in Exodus we have, "I am the Lord thy God." Jesus begins his prayer, "Our Father." In our modern idiom adapted to the mentality of this age, we say, "God is the only presence and the only power," but it is the old, old message, the old, old Truth.

Now, when God spoke to Moses out of the burning bush, He said, "I AM THAT I AM." And He said, "Thus shalt thou say unto the children of Israel, I AM hath sent me." This states, as clearly as can be done in limited language, the nature of God.

You cannot define God. To define means to limit, to make finite. When you say that a thing is red you mean it is not blue or green. When you say a thing is square you are implying that it is not round, and so forth. Any definition, any description, is a limitation if it is to be useful. However, God is infinite and you cannot define God. Spinoza said, "To define God is to deny Him." And so the Bible does not attempt to define God.

How different are the theologies. All the theologies, from the most ancient times down to the most recent, have been men's intellectual attempts to define God. Their intentions were to do that but in practice they usually analyzed themselves unconsciously and wrote their own characters into their definitions.

The Bible does not try to do that. The Bible teaches metaphysics and says that God is I AM THAT I AM. What does that mean? In the very same verse, God says to Moses, "Thou shalt say unto the children of Israel, I AM hath sent me."

I Am. But what is I Am? It is your true being. It is your real nature, your real self and nobody else, because no one else can say I Am for you. Only you can say I Am. That is your real identity, the Presence of God in you, the Indwelling Christ. That is you, and whatever you attach to I Am with conviction, that you are and that you have.

I Am is the fact of existence, and to know that gives you all power. When you have to go and tackle the "Egyptians" and your heart turns to water within you, and you say to yourself, "I cannot do this," "I am not adequate," "There is no way," then remember your true identity and say to the "Egyptians," "I AM hath sent me," and the road will open and you will surmount your difficulties.

Now, God spoke of Himself to Moses and said, "I AM THAT I AM," and that is the Bible's way of saying that God is pure, unconditioned Being. God does not sit on a throne in heaven. That is a figure of speech—a very beautiful one, if you like. God does not sit on a throne in heaven. There is no throne in heaven. If God could sit down, he would have legs and could wear shoes, and to suggest that is to bring the thing down to absurdity. The throne is the symbol of power. God is pure Spirit, Infinite Creative Life, Infinite Mind, Infinite Intelligence. God is pure, unconditioned Being.

When the Bible says that God talked to Moses out of the burning bush, it does not mean that God stood a little way off and talked to Moses as man to man. No, it was the Presence of God within Moses, as God is within you, Who taught him these things. In the Bibles of the seventeenth and eighteenth centuries there would be a picture of a very fierce-looking man in sandals and a long robe and huge beard, talking with Moses. Moses was represented as a much smaller man but dressed in the same way—two men talking, which of course is childish. God talked with Moses through the intuitive sense as he talks to men and women today who pray for His guidance.

God is I AM THAT I AM, and you are I Am, and you make your destiny and your own fate by the things that you attach to that I Am, for that is what you really believe about yourself. If you give credence to fear by saying, "I am afraid," then you are destroying yourself. Every time you entertain a pang of fear, or jealousy, or a thought of criticism, every time you speak an unkind word to anyone, and much more so if you say it about them when they are not present, you are definitely shortening and destroying your life. You are definitely breaking down your cells. You are making your body more sensitive to pain.

Nor do we lose a grain of good. Nobody can keep it away from you. Every time you say, "I am one with God," you are improving your life. Every time you refuse to be bullied by fear, every time you follow the highest you know, and put your trust in God, you are lengthening your life, improving your health, and making it more difficult for disease to attack you.

CHAPTER 5

Pocket Gods and Graven Images

> Thou shalt not make unto thee any graven image, or any
> likeness of any thing that is in heaven above, or that is in
> the earth beneath, or that is in the water under the earth:
>
> Thou shalt not bow down thyself to them, nor serve
> them: for I the Lord thy God am a jealous God, visiting
> the iniquity of the fathers upon the children unto the third
> and fourth generation of them that hate me;
>
> And showing mercy unto thousands of them that love
> me, and keep my commandments.
>
> EXODUS 20:4–6

I T is true that God is One and that we should not make idols. A primitive people needed to be told that because they were very much given to making idols of a palpable sort. They would cut off the bough of a tree and carve it into something like a man or an animal, or they would pick up a stone they liked, and worship that. We more sophisticated people sometimes wonder why, but when we consider the mental processes of the primitive man and his simple mental

reactions to his surroundings, we can begin to understand why, when fear struck and he was filled with anxi-
ety and suspense, it was natural for him to cling to
something outside of himself. So he built an idol to worship.

Moses had to tell his people not to do that. Of course,
they went on doing it to some extent anyway. You remember the story of the Golden Calf, and there were
other instances; but he told them not to.

I think when most people reread the Commandments
or go to church and see them written up somewhere,
they think to themselves, "Well, the First Commandment
is very important, but the second one, well, of course
that is out of date. That does not apply any more. People
do not make images and bow down and worship them
in these days." But when we look a little further we find
that that is not the case; and if each one of us will look into
his heart, we will find, perhaps to our surprise, that we
have made a good many images, a good many heathen
gods, and that every day of our lives we bow down and
worship them.

However, they are not so obvious and so palpable as
the gods of the ancients. You know in the ancient world
they used to make enormous images. The Egyptians and
the Babylonians, later on the Greeks and the Romans,
had large statues in their temples and then they had small
copies that they used to have in other places or carry
around with them. The Greeks naturally made them very
beautiful. The statues, the idols of the Greeks, have served
as our standards of beauty ever since—their Apollo, their
Venus, their Hercules, and so on. Other nations have
made them very ugly. Many of the Hindu idols are ap-
pallingly ugly. Many of the Egyptian gods seem curious to

us—gods with heads of hawks, gods with heads of cats and lions, and so forth. Even the most primitive savages have made themselves little idols, things formed of mud or clay, or carved out of a piece of wood.

Well, we do not do these things, but whenever we give power to anything but God, we are making that thing into a graven image, even though it is not a palpable image of wood or stone. Whenever we give power to anything but God we are making a graven image.

I am not saying that you must not admire or like something. All true liking, admiring, and joy is the expression of God. When you see a beautiful sunset or when you see a beautiful statue, the Winged Victory, for example, you should enjoy that and love it, knowing that it is the beauty and life and joy of God shining through it. But that is not making an image of it. You are not giving any power to it.

However, there are many things in life that we do give power to. For example, we give power to our ailments, particularly if it is a favorite ailment. I know that people laugh at that but I am sure we all know people who say, "My rheumatism," and they say it quite lovingly. Been with them a long time! They are rather fond of it! Has become a conversation piece! Others say, "My indigestion. You know there are very few things I would dare to eat," etc. We are making a graven image of these things. We are giving them power and we cannot heal them. It is only when we take power away from them that we can heal them.

Many people worship the planets. In the Bible, people were very carefully told not to worship the sun, moon, and stars. There again, you might say, "Well, today nobody would dream of doing that." Are you so sure? I have known people who crawled through life under the foolish fear of the planet Saturn. They say, "I was going to apply for a position this week, but I knew there was no use," and you ask them why, and they say, "Well, you know Saturn is against me this month." Unquestionably is! No doubt about it! He has made a graven image of it. Had he never heard of Saturn or Mars or Jupiter, he would have applied for the position and gotten it.

Often we make a graven image of ourselves. Now, I do not mean through vanity. That happens too, but people often make a graven image of themselves through depreciating themselves. You can be and do something very fine, the thing that God meant you to do, if you will get what I sometimes call the Mental Equivalent* for it. And if you say you cannot, no opportunity and so on, you are saying, "I am so important that God who made the universe cannot do anything about me. He can do anything else. Changed all these people in the Bible we read about, but when he gets around to me He is phased." You are making a graven image.

Then there are some people who are very self-righteous and egotistical. Well, they are also making a graven image of themselves. Selfishness is bad but neglecting yourself is also bad. The right thing always turns out to be a mean, as the Greeks said, between two extremes. There is a happy medium. Neglecting prayer is bad, but praying all day is bad, too.

There is an amusing story told about a famous Victorian divine, the great Bishop Wilberforce. Bishop Samuel Wilberforce was quite an eminent man in mid-Victorian

* See booklet, "The Mental Equivalent" (Unity School, Lee's Summit, Mo.).

and later days. He was a remarkable person because his friends tell us he experienced a religious conversion late in life, long after he was a clergyman. All through his life he was highly respected, but people thought he was rather self-righteous, rather formal. How can I put it? To use New York slang, he was spiritually highhat. Conversions usually come in youth. It is not often that men's or women's characters or dispositions change after thirty unless they get a divine contact, and he did, and quite late, and everybody noticed the change for the better.

However, after that he used to tell this story about himself. He said that one night, some years before his conversion, he was thinking of the wickedness of the world, and it bothered him. And he said, of course there was some self-righteousness there too. But he was bothered with the wickedness of the people, especially in London, the wickedness of those people in London—so unlike himself! And then he thought of the wickedness of people in general. The whole mass of humanity were terrible and God would surely punish them. He thought some awful thing would happen if he did not do something about it. So he decided to stay up all night to try to save the world. You see the heart was good, but you could not say that about the head. A warm heart should always be balanced by a cool head. So he decided to stay up all night to see if he could save the world from the doom it so thoroughly deserved. He knelt down and hour after hour besought God not to destroy the world. And he said that about the middle of the night God spoke to him, and said, "Go to bed now, Sam, I will take charge of the universe for the rest of the night."

He had made a graven image of himself, but when he got his divine contact, God destroyed that.

There is another kind of graven image that people sometimes make. You will remember that when Moses appeared before Pharaoh, the Bible says, "The Lord hardened Pharaoh's heart." That is one of the key points of the Bible. It puzzles many thoughtful people, and ought to puzzle everyone until he understands it. How can a good God harden Pharaoh's heart? And if He does, how can you blame Pharaoh? Suppose God made a man go out and shoot somebody. How can you blame that man for it and send him to the electric chair? You have to face up to these things. The Bible is the most important of all books, and you have to understand it. Running away from Bible problems means that in your heart you do not think the Bible is reliable.

Now this problem crops up right through the Bible from beginning to end—where God is spoken of as hurting someone. God has never hurt anybody and never will. To get near to God means that our body is healed, we get peace of mind, and we get harmony. Never has any kind of suffering or punishment come from God.

Whenever we think wrongly, we bring punishment on ourselves; but that is because punishment is the natural result of thinking wrongly, acting wrongly—perhaps not intentionally, maybe through ignorance—and the law carries it out. For example, if you say that you are not afraid of electricity, and then you touch a high voltage electric wire, you will be seriously injured if not killed. You will not have done anything wicked. You will merely have been very silly through lack of knowledge of the law. And when we break the laws of God through lack of knowledge, the results come in the same way.

"The Lord hardened Pharaoh's heart." That does not mean the Lord did it. Often in the Bible the word *Lord* means "law." Often if you read "law" where it says "Lord" you get the true idea.

It was Pharaoh's own understanding of what he called God that hardened his heart. Pharaoh was a pagan, and a pagan is a person who worships a false god, someone who has a pocket god as Pharaoh had. Pharaoh worshiped a god who was just a big man who lived in the sky and was awfully like Pharaoh himself, and that god used to get mad now and again and treat his enemies the way Pharaoh treated his. That god had all the weaknesses and meanness Pharaoh had. It was a projection of Pharaoh himself.

You know that many people today make the same mistake. Haven't you heard people who say that God will punish someone who does not do what pleases them? "I know God will punish my daughter because she married a man I do not approve of at all." "I know God will punish my son because he did not come into my business." God is always going to punish someone who does not do the thing that these people want. If you do what they want, God will be awfully pleased with you; and if you do not, God will surely punish you. Well, that is a pocket god, and that is what Pharaoh worshiped, and that is what hardened his heart.

So when you read that the Lord hardened Pharaoh's heart, it was Pharaoh's idea of the Lord, Pharaoh's idea of the Law of Being that hardened his heart.

Why did Judas go wrong? Did God make Judas go wrong? You know He did not. Did Jesus make him go wrong? Of course he did not. It was Judas giving way to the lower instead of the higher. In other words, the Lord hardened the heart of Judas in that sense. The heart of Judas was set upon material things, and he attached himself to Jesus in the beginning because he thought Jesus was going to build a great material kingdom. When he saw that Jesus was not going to build a worldly kingdom, he began to plot against him. All those ideas in the mind of Judas were his idea of God and of himself, and those are the things that hardened his heart.

That has happened to all of us at some time or other, that our false idea of God has hardened our hearts. It is so easy to see where Pharaoh is wrong, but Pharaoh is every one of us at some time or other. Every character in the Bible represents a state of consciousness, and although none of us has had all of them, we have had many of them.

There are times when you have been Abraham, when you have had great faith in God. There have been times when you have been Jacob wrestling with the angel to get your divine contact. There have been times when you have been Moses, and now and again, probably, though I hate to say it, you have been Pharaoh. And you were Pharaoh at any time in your life when you were trying to pretend to yourself or to others that God wanted what you wanted, that God did not like what you did not like, and that God was going to fix up everything as you wanted it. When you did that, you did not have the true God at all. You had made a graven image. You had a pocket god.

If you forget God and worship graven images of any kind, you are going to suffer. You can demolish a stone statue; you can burn a wooden one. The way to destroy mental images is to stop thinking of them and giving them power. Turn to God and He never fails.

Well then, this Commandment goes on to say, "For I the Lord thy God am a jealous God." This is very important, but we must remember that these words in the Bible are used in a technical sense. To begin with, our version of the Bible, the King James Version, is by far the best.

Nevertheless, it is written in the English of over four hundred years ago. It was published in 1611, and was a little archaic even then, because it was founded on earlier versions. Also we must remember—this is much more important—that all the great religious and occult truths (some occult truths are not religious and some religious truths are not occult) have to be given in symbol and allegory. Why? Because the truth about spiritual things cannot be put directly into everyday language. Everyday language was invented for the human mind, for the intellect and the feelings, but the spirit is something else. So for spiritual things, we have to have the new tongue, as Jesus called it. In order to give out a spiritual experience, to talk about it, to give it to other people as Moses did, we have to use the everyday language that is used for three-dimensional, intellectual, material things. In order to bridge the two—the infinite or spiritual, and the limited intellectual—we have to use the language of allegory and symbol.

So when Moses says God is a jealous God, he does not mean that God is jealous like a man. Jealousy, I suppose, is one of the meanest passions of the human heart, and to imagine that God could suffer from jealousy is only silly. It does not mean that. But it does mean that if you are going to worship God, God must have first place. He positively will not play second fiddle to anyone or anything else. The trouble with many pious people is that they want God to play second fiddle. They do not always realize it that way, but it is true. In their consciousness, God can be vice-president, but the presidency they keep for themselves—and it is generally understood, I believe, that the office of vice-president is more ornamental and honorable than actual.

So the Bible uses the word *jealous* in the sense that if you give power to anything but God, you have lost God altogether.

People have begun to realize this better nowadays because of the progress of natural science. Take sterilization, for instance. It is only seventy or eighty years now that surgeons have been sterilizing their knives. Pasteur began it. Prior to that, the nurse or the attendant breathed on the knife, rubbed it on his sleeve, and handed it to the doctor—that is, if they were particular! If they were not, the doctor just plunged the knife in as it was. Why not? A knife is a knife. I remember, when I was a child in London, hearing one or two very elderly surgeons speak of the things they had seen before Pasteur's time, before the Crimean War, when Florence Nightingale got to work. Today it would be incredible to most people. Even long after Pasteur's time, the attendants would sterilize the knives carefully and then lay them down anywhere, not realizing that when a thing is sterilized nothing must touch it. It was no good scolding them or firing them; the next lot would do the same thing. It took a generation to make people realize that when a thing is sterilized it must be sterilized and then isolated.

Well now, it has taken us all these thousands of years to realize the same sort of thing about God; that if we adulterate the thought of God with anything else, we have lost God altogether. And so the Bible uses the word *jealous*. We know that a jealous person will not allow anybody else even to look at his beloved. Some men are even jealous of their fathers, mothers, brothers, or sisters. They do not even want their wives to visit their own families, they are so jealous. Well, the Bible takes that because it is a thing everybody knows about, and applies it to God, to give us an idea of the utter and utter and utter exclusiveness with which we must worship God. If you give power or place to anything but God, you have lost God altogether. You cannot have a percentage of God. Either God is the only power, or nothing at all.

Regarding visiting the iniquity of the fathers upon the children unto the third and fourth generation, that has frightened many people who peep into the Bible here and there without studying it carefully. In particular, they have applied it to what is called hereditary diseases, those that are supposed to run in the family. One of them is gout, for instance. It is generally believed that if your father or grandfather had gout, you will probably have it, but if they did not have it, you probably will not. These people overlook the fact that the Bible also says, in the 18th chapter of Ezekiel, that this law is repealed. If anyone is afraid of hereditary influence on the grounds of what the Bible says, let him turn to that chapter and he will see that there it says that this law has been repealed and is over with.

No children are ever punished for the sins of their fathers or anyone else. We are never punished by or for anything except our *own* mistakes in the present or the past, perhaps the distant past.

You do not inherit disease from your family or your parents or grandparents. Now, I am perfectly well aware that certain disease seem to run in families—much fewer, however, than the layman thinks. The number of diseases that the up-to-date physician would call hereditary is far less than, say, a doctor would have done thirty or forty years ago. I know that certain things seem to run in families, but they are not inherited. The soul before it was born had that tendency and was steered to that family because like attracts like. The stork never makes a mistake. It was not coincidence and it was not heredity. If you go into a Presbyterian church today you will find that nearly all the people there are Presbyterians. If you go into a Baptist church, they are nearly all Baptists. That is not heredity; neither is it coincidence. They are drawn there because of similarity of thought and religion.

In this phrase about the iniquities of the fathers, it does not literally mean one's children or grandchildren. In the symbology of the Bible, you are a father, and your children are your works, the works of your hands, of your brain—people sometimes refer to an author's book, or a man's invention, as his brain child—the things you produce, and the things you do. These are your children, and if you do not give all power to God, you will lack inspiration and guidance, and all your activities will suffer, to the third and fourth generation.

In the Commandments, as I have said, there are various layers of meaning and instruction. The Bible is always concerned with the individual soul, and so in the deeper symbology of the Bible, our ancestors mean our selves of yesterday, our selves when they were younger than they are now. And our children and grandchildren mean our selves of tomorrow and next week and next year.

You are the children of that man or woman of a few years ago, or twenty or thirty years ago. And tomorrow, and ten years from now, the "you" of that time will be the child or grandchild of the "you" of today.

So this text says that our iniquity or mistakes of today, we shall have to pay for tomorrow, or the next day, or next year, because "we hate God," which in the Bible sense means those that do not seek Him, do not love

Him. This gives us the key to wiping out past mistakes and thereby the results of them, by turning to God in prayer. When we make mistakes or think negatively, when we sin as our orthodox friends say, we shall have to pay for them unless we turn to God in prayer, and seek to do His will. This is loving God, and the Bible says that God will show mercy to them that love Him and keep his Commandments. That is the forgiveness of sins. When you get sufficient realization of the presence of God, you will not want to make that mistake again, and then you will not be punished because you will have become a different man. The Bible always finishes by teaching us the love and goodness and mercy of God.

CHAPTER 6

The True Witness

Thou shalt not bear false witness against thy neighbour.
EXODUS 20:16

W E have now reached the place where we can
go deeper into this study of the laws of life.

I am not sure but that this Commandment,
"Thou shalt not bear false witness," is the most important of all the Commandments when we properly understand it.

First, the obvious meaning is very important although
it is only the beginning—do not tell lies about people. I
suppose we were all taught that as small children. Do not
say that Tommy took the cookies when you took them. Do
not say you took them to cover him up. That is pretty obvious but it is not always observed, you know. Even the
very best people, as they are called, often bear false witness against their neighbors.

Take politics, for example. Many people have a "slight"
tendency to excessive criticism of the other side! Have
you noticed it—especially around election time? Now

that is a serious matter because if it is not checked, democracy may become impossible. In democratic countries, if a candidate for office is going to be vilified and accused of every crime under the sun, if, as soon as a man stands, or runs—in England you stand for Parliament but in America you run for Congress (difference in tempo, you know)—if, as soon as a man runs for mayor, or governor, or senator, or president, if he is going to be accused of every foul thing, what will happen? Decent, sensitive men will not run for public office. Only the toughest people will do it. If the men who are really qualified in every way, with a high sense of honor, are going to be vilified like this, they will not run for office. So it is very important not to attack people in politics in that unfair way. I do not mean that they should not be criticized. You can say Jones's policy is bad, that it will ruin the country, but not that Jones is a crook or that he beats his wife, when you have seen Mrs. Jones and know quite well it is probably the other way around!

A generation or two ago it was the custom for ministers of religion to vilify all the other churches. The Episcopalians were told just where the Baptists were going, and most Baptists did not need to be told where the Episcopalians were going—they knew! The only thing they agreed on was what would happen to the Presbyterians and Roman Catholics. Read some of the old sermons. When I started in this work I read some of the old-time sermons of Spurgeon, Beecher, Wendell Phillips, and the lesser fry. Some of the things they said were surprising. If you were to read some of John Wesley's sermons, which are not printed nowadays, you would be surprised, and I am a great admirer of Wesley. Some of the things that were said then would be impossible today.

We have to apply this principle of not bearing false witness right throughout our lives. It is very important in practice because whatever you say about another person will happen to yourself. That is the law of Karma. If you lie about another person—that is an unpleasant word but I am using it because it is the right word—someone will lie about you. Jesus says so in the 7th chapter of Matthew, verses 1 and 2.*

What about slander, backbiting, gossip? There has been a terrific amount of suffering and injustice in the world caused just by malicious gossip, usually quite untrue. Of course, anybody on the spiritual path, with the slightest desire for spiritual progress, will not indulge in gossip. Remember that the person who listens is just as bad as the person who speaks it. If there is no listener, to that extent there can be no gossip.

Some preachers say that we shall be punished by God for bearing false witness, but in the Truth teaching we know that we shall be punished by the Law of Being— as ye mete, so shall it be meted unto you. I just mention that in passing.

Now, all these things are the obvious or surface meaning of this Commandment, "Thou shalt not bear false witness."

The real or fundamental meaning is that you always express what you are. You cannot be one thing and express another. Emerson says, "What you are shouts so loudly that I cannot hear what you say." It is a wonderful saying. We are always witnessing to what we are. Sometimes we can fool people for a time, we can throw a bluff for a while, but sooner or later what we are comes out, and

*See also *The Sermon on the Mount* (Harper & Row), p. 117.

sensible people mentally place us about where we belong.

So again, "Thou shalt not" really means "You cannot"—you cannot permanently bear false witness. As long as we witness to error, we are bearing false testimony, and our business is to witness to the Truth of Being.

What is the Truth of Being? The Truth of Being is health, harmony, joy, freedom of expression, dominion. Are we witnessing to that? Not one of us completely, as yet. We all have our limitations. There is not one of us in the world today who does not have his difficulties, his problems, his faults of character. So to that extent each one of us is bearing false witness, and it is because of this that we have our troubles and difficulties. We have dominion over all things but we are witnessing to limitation, poverty, depression, and fear.

The very rich people are often just as full of fear as the poor people, and so they are really impoverished. I suppose, on the average, 50 percent of the people who consult me have all the money they can use, and 50 percent are hard up. I think, on the whole, the 50 percent who are hard up are better off—for this reason: when a man is hard up, he always thinks that if he could only get hold of some money, he would be all right. But the other 50 percent do not even have that hope. They already have the money and are miserable in spite of that. The poor man fears his limitation. He cannot buy the things he wants. The rich man fears he may lose his money, or anarchists or communists get into power and take it away. So the rich man too is witnessing to limitation.

People are also witnessing to mental limitation. Men and women, even today, do not realize more than 5 percent of their potentialities. Just as they are today, without learning a single thing more, without more power or understanding, without reading another book, there is not one who could not go right out and do some very wonderful worthwhile things. But they do not think so. There is not one who could not go out and do something far finer than he has ever dreamed of, if he had the self-confidence, determination, and vision. Where there is no vision, the people perish. They are bearing false witness.

The Bible says, "Thou shalt not bear false witness," but so long as we are demonstrating or expressing limited bodies, sickness, and what we call middle age or old age, or are in possession of anything but perfect health, perfect freedom, perfect happiness, we are bearing false witness. That is why I am not sure but that this is the most important of all the Commandments.

Our bounden duty is to bear true witness to our neighbor. What are we showing him? All right. Let each one of us go and look in the glass. Get by yourself, have a good look, not one of those peeks you see people having in trains and restaurants, but have a good look at yourself in the glass, and say, "Now, is this a witness to an eternal, divine being?" Do we really look like Greek gods and goddesses? Not all of us. Not our friends, at any rate! And the Greek gods or goddesses would be a very limited thing compared to divine man.

Let us look at our surroundings, and say, "Am I bearing true witness to God's man? Am I surrounded by delightful, interesting, fine people?" If you are, you are bearing true witness, but most people, I am sure, are not quite satisfied. They think their friends, their relatives, and their associates leave much to be desired.

The true witness is the full expression of God's man. You will be bearing true witness to your neighbor when you are regenerated in soul, for when the soul is regenerated, the body will be regenerated, too.

What is regeneration? Generation means creating: re-generation means re-creating. It does not mean patching up the old hulk. It means generating or creating a new body. The goal of the Jesus Christ teaching is re-generation, and anyone who misses that misses the Jesus Christ message. People think they have it when they use the name of Jesus, but they do not necessarily have his teaching. You may think you get a thing without having it at all.

Once a bishop traveling in Africa visited a native village in the middle of the Congo where there was a missionary settlement, to baptize the native population who had been made into apparently sound, orthodox Christians. He questioned them through an interpreter on the catechism and what they had learned. They all had the answers pat and the bishop was greatly edified. So he confirmed them. That night he was awakened by a light outside and a strong smell of burning flesh. He and the missionary looked out and found that the converts had built a bonfire and were sacrificing two pigeons to the white god who had recently confirmed them. So you see how much of the prayer book they had really absorbed. To them the bishop was just one more heathen god. They did not have the thing at all.

Most of us have been just as far away as that from the Jesus Christ teaching, because we have overlooked regeneration. The goal of the Christian religion is not to die in the odor of sanctity and be buried with a fine church funeral—it is regeneration, and unless we are trying to regenerate, we are missing the Christ message.

What does regeneration mean? It means the building of a new soul, not correcting the old one. You know that if there is an old house that is rather rickety, you can put a few new clapboards on it, a few more tiles on the roof, a coat of paint, and maybe put in a new stove. But you are patching up the old house. The way of regeneration is to pull down the old house, clean the foundation and build a new one. When you begin to do that in your spiritual life you are practicing the Jesus Christ teaching.

Nothing you do to the body can change the body fundamentally. You can patch it up, yes, but only a change in the soul will change the body fundamentally, for the body is but the outpicturing of the soul. I always recommend people to be reasonable and careful about diet and exercise and all those things. I think we should eat in accordance with the best knowledge of the present day. I think we should take proper exercise. I think bathing and open windows and fresh air are fine habits. However, not one of those things will regenerate you. They will make the best of you as you are today, but they will not make a new man or woman of you. These things are worthwhile but they will not regenerate you.

Regeneration goes beyond all these outer things and changes the soul. When you change the soul, automatically the body begins to change. The flesh changes, the skin changes, the blood vessels and the nerves and the bones change.

Regeneration must begin with a change in the soul, not with anything in the outer world. Of course, we must change our conduct. The Israelites were told to wash their clothes and prepare themselves. Figuratively we must wash our clothes. If we are doing anything wrong, we must quit. A man who has false scales in his shop, or a professional man who cheats his clients, must stop that. A man who is conscious of any kind of moral fault must clean that up.

It means that if you want any spiritual understanding, if you want healings and other things, you must start by

cleansing your life. You must positively try to stop thinking negatively. You will not do that in a day or a week if you
have a habit, but you must be trying. You must try to stop
speaking critically. If there is something in your life that
you know is wrong, you must try to get rid of it. Perhaps
you will not succeed at once because the habit is strong.
For instance, a man who has been in the grip of drink
might not be able to do so at first, but he must try.

That is "washing your clothes" and getting ready for a
new spiritual experience. That is the real meaning of the
Christian baptism. Baptism is a symbol of washing or
cleansing, and when we want seriously to adapt ourselves
to the spiritual life we have to start cleansing ourselves
as well as we can.

In the later centuries it became a superstition. People
thought that if you were baptized you could be saved and
if you were not baptized then you could not be saved.
That was making a ritual of a beautiful symbol.

When John was baptizing people, he said to them, if
you want to find God, if you want peace of mind, you
must start by cleaning yourself up. John the Baptist was a
wonderful person, but we do not feel there was very much
love in him. He did not have much patience with people. He saw a crowd of people once and he called them
a group of vipers. You could not imagine Jesus doing that.
Jesus had infinite love and compassion. Still, John taught
the truth that you must begin with a cleansing.

That was why Jesus said that no one born of woman is
higher than John the Baptist, by which he meant no ordinary natural man, but he also said that the least in the
kingdom of heaven is greater than he, by which he meant
that the person who turns to God and lets God do it
through him, will be infinitely more than the person who
is just trying by himself, even though he tries his very best.

So that cleansing process is necessary, and if anyone says that he does not find it easy, who does? But if you say, "I recognize now that I am full of imperfections, perhaps some serious ones, but with the help of God I will clean them up," then God comes and begins to do it.

Regeneration ultimately means realizing your oneness with God—realizing it. Realizing means making real, and you do that by thinking of God, by believing in your oneness with Him, by revising your ideas and views on all things. You have got to revise your opinions about everything, beginning with God and working right down to the devil. Do not forget anything. You were probably brought up to think of the devil as a person with horns and tail and dressed in crimson tights, something like Mephisto in *Faust*. All right. Revise your idea right now. The devil is really your own fears, your own doubts, your own selfishness. Revise your idea of God as a big man up in the sky. Revise your idea of the Bible, and of fellow man.

Revise your idea of your business, whatever it is. Do you think your business is merely a way for making a living, getting money from other people? Most of so-called big business has long since revised its ideas about business. Most large corporations now realize that their primary function is to be of service to the community and to the country. Often, however, the individual looks upon his business or his job as just a means for making a living. Well, revise that idea too. It is not that at all.

Revise your idea of social relationships. Revise your idea of time. Remember that God is outside the calendar and that you dwell in eternity.

I mentioned earlier that we should revise our idea about our mental capacity, and I repeat it. There is not one of us who could not go out and do something fine, if he had sufficient true confidence and vision and courage.

So we must revise all our ideas. This is bearing true witness, and when we bear true witness to our neighbor of what we are, we change him as well. No one person can regenerate without helping the whole world to some extent. When Jesus overcame death, he made it possible for us to do it. When Moses dematerialized, he made it easier for the rest of the world to do the same thing.

So you should bear true witness to your neighbor. This is the truth about you. You are a divine being. You are not a limited thing, weighing so many pounds, so many inches high. You are a divine being. You are spiritual and perfect. You were never born and you will never die. We saw a picture of you when you first appeared on this plane some years ago, but that was not your beginning. You are living in eternity here and now. You are one with God, and potentially you express every quality of God.

When we really *know* these things, we shall be bearing true witness. We shall not have to stay here much longer, and unless we want to, we need never come back, for the true witness will never go.

CHAPTER 7

Expressing What You Are

Thou shalt not kill.

EXODUS 20:13

I have said two or three times that the Commandments are to be taken at their face value and that they are binding as such, but that is only the beginning. As rules of conduct, the Commandments are "Thou shalt nots," just as you see written up, "No smoking" or "No thoroughfare." But when you get behind the surface meaning, then "Thou shalt not" becomes "Thou canst not."

So this Commandment, "Thou shalt not kill," is really and fundamentally an expression of the cosmic law that you cannot kill, and the sooner you find that out the better.

We are always trying to kill. Not people, of course; we leave that to the gangsters. At least we do not kill people suddenly although some do try to kill others slowly. However, this Commandment is here to tell us that we cannot

kill, and to think that we can kill anything is to fool ourselves and to lay up trouble for ourselves that will have to
be met and wiped out some time or other.

You cannot kill. Nothing ever dies from the outside.
No one can kill you. No one can kill your character. No
one can kill your peace of mind. No one can kill your
business, or your reputation, or anything that is yours.
You can, but nobody else can. No man or woman was
ever yet destroyed from the outside.

You need not fear your enemies if you have any. You
need not cast a thought to them—unless it be a good
thought—for they are absolutely powerless to hurt you.
No one can do that but yourself.

No corporate body was ever yet destroyed from the
outside. No political party was ever yet destroyed from
the outside. No church was ever yet destroyed from the
outside. On the contrary, it has been a well-known saying
in history that the blood of the martyrs is the seed of the
church. The more a particular religion is persecuted the
stronger it becomes. Nevertheless, many great religions
have withered and died. There was a time when the great
Egyptian religion was the great church of the world, the
most powerful, the best organized, and all the thought-
less people of that day said, "It will last forever." Where is
it now?

Then there was the great Babylonian religion, a wonderful thing, all mixed up with the natural science of the
day. People said, "This is the truth. This will last forever."
Where is it today? None of these was destroyed from the
outside. You cannot kill.

The same thing is true with a business. A great business is built up. Everyone in the country gets to know
about it. It goes on for a couple or even three or four

generations, and then it disappears—suddenly or gradually, as a rule. What happened to it? Competition did not kill it. It was not a rival that put it out of business. Nevertheless, the life went out of that firm. Perhaps the grandfather had built it up and the father made it a great success. Then the grandson? Well, he just did not have what is necessary, and so the business gradually fell apart. There is an old proverb that says it is three generations from shirtsleeves to shirtsleeves. And so the thing withers away, but nothing is ever destroyed from the outside.

That is a wonderful thought. I wish every boy and girl in high school could be taught that. I wish that someone in every high school would take a quarter of an hour to explain to the boys and girls in a simple way that no one can hurt them but themselves.

For instance, there is a perfectly dreadful custom of taking a census in school to see who is the most popular, or who is most likely to succeed. That has an appalling effect on many of the students. It does not really matter whether they are popular or not. They should be told that nothing that anyone else can do to them can really hurt them. I wish that someone would say to them, "You will meet critics, competitors, and even enemies perhaps. You may have to work under people who you think are inimical to your welfare, but not one of these people can hurt you in the least. You can only express in experience your own true sense of what you really are. However, you can destroy yourself. If you are going out into the world and be very foolish and make stupid mistakes, neglect your work, be dishonest or unreliable, or if you are going to forget God, then you will come to grief. You may make a lot of money for a while, or be looked up to as a very important person, but you will come to shipwreck. However,

it will be from yourself. No one outside can hurt you."
Boys and girls of that age are very "quick on the uptake."
That kind of teaching would change their whole lives.

I know not how many people waste their lives in thinking how they are being hurt, or damaged, or injured by
other people, how they are kept back because other people are against them, how good they could be, and the
marvelous things they could do, if it were not for others.
It is a kind of self-drugging. So long as people believe
that, they get nowhere. They cannot progress. As soon
as they know that nobody can hurt them, they are free to
overtake any mistakes, and to be and do the thing they
want.

That is the inner metaphysical meaning of this Commandment, which has been known to the occult students
of all ages. However, it is only in the present age that it is
being given out to the general public. For many reasons
that is so, one being that they would not have understood it or believed it in former generations. They would
have said, "That is nonsense he is making up. He is very
dangerous. It is not the accepted teaching. We had better burn him alive, just in case." Thank God we can afford
to laugh at that now. There was a time not so long ago,
when it was no laughing matter to get new ideas out of the
Bible. Many a man has been burned alive for that very
thing—for daring to open the Bible and finding something in it that was not being officially taught. When the
Pilgrim Fathers came to this country to escape from that
very thing, one of the first things they did was to hang
three Quakers on Boston Common. The Pilgrims came
here for an open Bible themselves, but if anyone else
opened it he was hanged—just to learn him, as the school-
boy says.

Now, I do want to emphasize again that we cannot kill. Those who burnt alive the martyrs and reformers did not kill them. Nero did not kill Christianity. He had a good try but he did not kill it. You know what was done to the people; thrown to the wild beasts, burnt alive sometimes, and so forth. Then a long time afterward, there came an emperor who nearly destroyed Christianity with kindness. Constantine did not burn Christians or throw them to the lions, but he established Christianity as the state religion and made all the teachers state officials. That all but killed it—not quite, but nearly.

However, you cannot kill, and so it survived. And then Hus was murdered. Other people were murdered, but the Truth went on, because you can murder but you cannot kill. You know that if you murder a man, you do not kill him. He is as much alive as ever; sometimes more alive in death than he was in life. You cannot kill. Life goes on, and it is for us to see that not only does that life go on through us but that it goes on through us unimpeded, and that we make no effort to kill it. Many of us do try to kill the life in ourselves by disappointment and discouragement. A man is not doing the things that he hoped to do, or getting to the place where he hoped to get. He becomes discouraged. He says, "What's the use?" He is really trying to kill his soul, but he cannot do it.

Sometimes people do go so far as to kill the body. Then they find that they are more alive than ever, and will still have to come back and face the same problems that they tried to run away from.

Now the way to let your life live, and grow, and multiply is to seek for the Christ consciousness, which, in the beginning at any rate, is not some wonderful, mystical experience. That is not the beginning. That is getting

toward the end. The beginning of the Christ consciousness is what the Bible calls a humble and a contrite heart.
Does that sound rather old-fashioned and rather pious?
It does. But when you get below the surface meaning, it
has a wonderful psychological meaning. It is the humble mind that finds God; the humble heart that gets a
demonstration.

Well now, the way to God, which, of course, is the way
to the Christ consciousness, which means to cease trying to kill that wonderful thing within us, is to have that
true humility of spirit in which you say, "Lord, I believe;
help thou mine unbelief. I know very little but I know
enough to know that God is all, and that is all that matters. I know that is only the beginning because I know
that for God I need the new tongue. God does not speak
English or French or German or any human language,
neither Hebrew nor Greek (though the Bible was written in those languages). I need the new tongue, which
means a new heart, a change of outlook, a change of feeling. I know that God is Spirit. I know that God is expressed in simple things and simple ways—very profound,
the most profound of all, but very simple. I know that I
cannot find God if I think I am very important. If I get
that kind of swelled head, I have shut myself off from
God. If I feel that my limitations and my faults and my
weaknesses can keep me from God, I am shutting myself
away too, because in that way I am giving importance to
myself. If I have any feeling or resentment against other
people, if there is any human being in the world whom
I would like to see punished, or whose difficulty or whose
fault I would rejoice in, then I have shut myself away from
God, just as a man who burrows into a deep cave shuts
himself away from the daylight and cannot get it again

until he comes out. If I feel that anything else is worth having except a contact with God, I have shut myself off from God. If I really feel that there is anything that life can give me such as honors, public esteem, money, power, what you please; if I feel that anything like that can be more important than the search for God, I shall probably get my wish, and it will destroy me."

Anything you really want you can get. That is an old story in the Truth movement. When you look around the world and see how little most people get, it is because they do not know what they really want.

If you go into the five-and-ten, which is one of the most extraordinary enterprises in the world today, and wander around and around not knowing what you want, the manager may even get suspicious when he sees you lurking about. And then when he wants to know what he can do for you, and you say that, well, you really do not know, of course you won't get anything—unless it be an icy stare!

So it is with life. If you know what you want, you will probably get it, but you must be certain that you want the right things, for otherwise you may very well get them to your own damnation. Many people of fulfilled ambition find that they are eating Dead Sea fruit—the apple that rots in their mouths.

Now, we have our free will. We can make or mar our destiny, and if we allow ourselves to think that anything the world can offer is more worthwhile for a single moment than a contact with God, we shall get what we want, but we shall lose God. This is one of the very simple truths the Bible teaches. It is so simple that we miss it. Think of the lunatic maze of theology that has been drawn up through the centuries—I do not mean the Christian theologies only, but all the old theologies—that extraordinary maze in which the human mind has lost itself; and then realize that the truth about God is really simplicity itself. It is as simple and as universal as water. Water is the one thing that we cannot live without for very long, but the water of life we miss.

And so here in this extraordinary treatise on human nature and the search for God, Moses says that you cannot kill. People are always trying to kill, either themselves or their circumstances. A man gets to the point of realizing his weaknesses and baseness, and he thinks there is some quick mechanical way in which he can kill all that and be something different, perhaps by attending a church or by mechanical baptism. Many people for many centuries thought that by being baptized they could be utterly changed, but a very few days told a different story.

You must express your consciousness. If there is evil in it you will express that and have to meet it. The only way out is to get your contact with God. That does not kill; it transmutes. It takes base things and makes them fine. It takes away weakness and gives power. That is the first step to freedom, and there is not any other.

CHAPTER 8

Polarity

*Honour thy father and thy mother: that thy days may be
long upon the land which the Lord thy God giveth thee.*
EXODUS 20:12

I N our study of the Ten Commandments, spiritually interpreted, we have gotten to the Commandment that gives us practical instruction in prayer. We are taking a very wide and, I think, a very profound view of the Commandments, as Moses intended them to be taken.

Of course, it is true that you should respect your parents not for any other reason than that they are your parents. If your father is a wonderful man, you respect him for that, but you should respect him also just because he is your father. If your mother is a marvelous woman, you respect and admire her for that, but you should also respect her just because she is your mother. I suppose I am terribly old-fashioned but I think that we should respect our parents just because they are our parents, and I do not have much respect for anyone who does not. You should respect your parents even if they have any obvious faults, and you, as their child, have reason to know what their faults are.

Little children are the Recording Angel domesticated. Little pitchers have big ears, as the proverb says. Remember—those of you who are parents—that those little eyes and little ears are watching and listening day and night, not just when you are being parental and instructing them, and telling them that they must always be wise and just and true, and so forth. They do not pay much attention then, but they do pay attention at other times, when you have forgotten that they are around. Your children know all about you. They do not realize it when they are children, but as they grow up, it unfolds—they know their parents—and as a rule, they love them all the more.

So you must honor your parents, but that is just the very outer husk of the Commandment. Underneath it is instruction in divine metaphysics and prayer, because your real father and mother is God. (In some sections of the metaphysical movement they refer to God as Father-Mother God.)

When this Commandment says, "Honour thy father and thy mother," it brings in the two poles, the male and the female, and, of course, polarity is the motive power of the universe. Polarity is always present. That is why God is often described as a trinity. God is One, but if that One were undifferentiated, there would be no expression. To get activity, you must have the two poles, and these poles with their interaction produce a third thing. There is the Father, the Son, and the Holy Spirit.

Although God differentiates Himself through this principle of polarity, nevertheless God is One. So when this Commandment tells us to honor our father and our mother, it is telling us to recognize God as the only Cause, the only Presence, and the only Power, and that if we do that our days shall be long in the land—we shall have no troubles or difficulties.

If we would really recognize only One Cause, difficulties would not come into our lives. If, in the beginning, they did seem to do so, they would fade out quickly. Presently we would make the great demonstration and would not have to come back here at all unless we wanted to—if we really recognized that God is the only Presence and the only Power and the only Cause.

When we give power to anything else, as for example when we give power to the calendar, and say, "Well, of course, you know at my age," or "If I had had this chance at twenty; if I had known this at thirty," then we are not honoring our father and our mother, but we are giving power to the time belief, and everyone today knows that what we call time is an illusion. They do not put it that way but everybody knows that time is not the real thing our parents and grandparents thought it.

Sometimes we give power to matter, by saying, "There are laws of nature, you know. After all, you cannot change the law of gravity, or Boyle's law, or somebody else's law." Then we are not honoring our father and our mother— we are not honoring God.

Believing in time, and believing in the power of matter and decay, makes us old, and ultimately kills us. Giving power to matter and the laws of nature limits us in every way. Giving power to one another by saying, "I can't do thus and so in my life; I can't be what I want to be because I don't know the right people; I haven't influence," limits us too. It is acknowledging a second cause, and a second cause is idolatry. That attacks the First and Second Commandments, and trouble follows.

All the Commandments are really viewing the great Truth from different angles, for it is the One Truth. They all dovetail into one another. To break this Commandment, "Honour thy father and thy mother"—to have some power other than God—is dishonoring your parent who is God; it is also breaking the First Commandment; and it is also bearing false witness; and you can see too that it is attempting to steal something from God, and so forth and so on.

Now God is Father and Mother. The human parents are really foster parents. If parents would regard themselves in this true light as the guardians or foster parents of their children—the representatives of God—then they would be much better parents and they would have better children, and things would be much easier for them. It would save three-fourths of the wear and tear of parenthood.

If you say to yourself, "I have to think for John or Mary. I have to take care of them, provide for them, clothe them, and educate them; I have to try to give them in a package the wisdom it has taken me forty years to accumulate," you will wear yourself out, for you cannot really give your experience to another. But if you say, "No, I am the foster parent. I am the channel. That child is the child of God," then you will find it much easier to provide for the child financially, and it will be much easier to influence him for good with your prayers and with your advice.

Well now, God is the Father and the Mother, the only Cause, and to realize that God is the only Cause, in any place or condition where there is trouble, immediately begins to heal that difficulty. The truth about God is that God is the only Cause. Conditions have no power. It is ridiculous to say that prayer will not heal this condition

today when twenty days ago, or twenty years ago, it could
have healed it, but now it is too late; or to say, "God could
have got us out of this trouble before the judge's decision on Monday, but now that the decision has been
handed down God cannot do anything about it." Yet it is
that sort of argument, not put in exactly that way, that
destroys nine prayers out of ten. It is accepting power in
conditions, and there is no power in conditions.

There is no cause and effect in the material world.
Nothing ever happens in the material world as a result of
something that happened before in the material world.
Nothing has ever happened in the material world on
Tuesday as a consequence of what happened in the material world on Monday. It may seem to be so but it is
not. Always the picture in the material world is the outpicturing of the *state of mind at that moment,* and a man's
conditions on Monday are the expression of his mentality on Monday. His conditions on Wednesday are the expression of his mentality on Wednesday. They do not
follow from the outer conditions of Monday.

You say, "Well, suppose that a man on Monday is sentenced to a month in jail. Monday they put him in jail.
Tuesday he is in jail. Wednesday he is in jail. Isn't that
the result of what happened on Monday?"

No, it is not. Being sentenced on Monday was the outpicturing of the man's thought that led him to break the
law. His conditions on Wednesday must be the outpicturing of his convictions then. If he or someone for him
could change his mentality on Wednesday, he would be
released. I know that to the world this sounds crazy. But
after all, if God is the only Presence and the only Power,
the world, which is built on the belief that there are other
causes, must be crazy and it is. The world is not sane.
Look around the world today and ask yourself if it is sane.

The reason that there is war in the world is nothing but a belief in more causes than one. There does not have to be any war. Men do not have to cut one another's throats for the means whereby to live. There is enough of everything for everybody. Each and every one of us has access to infinite supply without taking from his neighbor.

There is no problem that can come to you or me that cannot be solved by realizing that there is only One Cause. Are you afraid? I do not need any answer. There is not one who is not afraid, at least to some degree. Some have more fear than others, some have less. That is the only difference. Should we be afraid if we really believed in only One Cause? Of course, we should not. All fear arises from believing in a second cause, which is idolatry. If we really believed there was only one Cause—and that One Cause must be good—then we should have no fear.

In these Ten Commandments Moses reminds us in various ways that it is the knowledge of the One Cause that gets us out of the land of Egypt, and out of the house of bondage.

That One Cause acts through you in your thought. You are a mental being. You are a thinker. The very word *man* means "a thinker." It is derived from the old Sanskrit word *manas* meaning "a thinker." Sanskrit is the great-grandfather of all the European languages. You are a thinker rather than a doer because what you do is only what you think. We do not like to face up to that sometimes. It can be very embarrassing. We like to think that we are rather nice people, but now and again we do things that are not so nice, and we like to think we can be nice notwithstanding. We cannot, because the deed is only the outer expression of the thought.

Now a good deal of nonsense has been taught in the metaphysical movement about the power of thought. To hear some people talk about the power of thought, you would think they could build the Eiffel Tower in their backyard tomorrow afternoon, just by the power of thought.

Thought has no power whatever unless it is accompanied by feeling. It is only the thought that you feel that demonstrates. The idea that every thought you think for a single moment is going to do something to you is childish, because it does not. You can readily see that if that were so humanity would just be nonexistent by now. Remember, that when you come into the metaphysical movement, it does not mean that you can check your hat at the door and your common sense with it. You must bring your common sense along. Anything that will not stand up to true logic and will not demonstrate in practice, must be wrong. Only those thoughts are demonstrated that are felt strongly. When you give a treatment (when you pray scientifically or affirmatively), if you feel it strongly, that treatment will be demonstrated, and all the obstacles in the world could not stop it. The gates of hell shall not prevail against it. On the other hand, if you are the finest person who ever walked, and you think a thought or give a treatment without feeling it, it is gone with the wind, and is heard of no more, because there must be the "father" and the "mother"—knowledge and feeling. The offspring is the demonstration or healing. There must always be feeling in order to effect a change or whatever it is that you are seeking to express. There must be polarity.

The law of polarity, which I have briefly touched on in this chapter, is one of those cosmic laws that are true to the farthest star, beyond the farthest nebula that we can see today and right up through the planes to the throne of God. For example, you cannot have an electric motor or dynamo without an armature and a field magnet. There must be polarity. In inorganic matter, there must be the proton and the electron, and in the organic world, there must be male and female.

That is what sex is, organic polarity. Of course, the world thinks of sex only on the lowest, the physical plane. But no statesman worthy of the name nowadays overlooks the fact that there are two sexes in the country, with their mentalities poised in different ways, male and female. In the old days, the state was built on the assumption that there were only men. Women were overlooked. As a reaction to that, I have heard some suffragists in London in the old days who felt that the creation of man was a mistake, and that the Almighty would have shown a good deal more wisdom if He had confined Himself to the superior sex! Most women did not feel that way, but some did. Of course, part of the social problem of today is adjusting that polarity, giving woman her true place. The early reformers made the mistake of saying that woman was exactly the same as man. There was no difference. The pioneers of women's freedom, two generations ago, took the line that there was no difference. That was silly. The true freedom of women, and the true opportunity for women, will come when we realize that a woman is a human being who is expressing as a woman in this particular life, as she has expressed as a man in previous lives and will again; that a man is a human being who is expressing as a man pro tempore, has been a woman in some other lives, and a man in others; and that the woman expression is fundamentally different from, but supplementary and complementary to, the man, and that man is fundamentally different, too.

America is the country above all others where woman is coming into her true place. In all sorts of ways women get an opportunity and a freedom in America that they do not get in the older countries, not, remember, because men keep it from them. In the Old World, it is not that men keep freedom from women. The mischief is that women in Europe and Asia for the most part do not really want it.

Recently I was thinking over what might be the most striking or significant thing I had seen in America. I have been in every state of the Union, and I have seen almost all the things that are shown to visitors and a great many things that are not, which I have dug out for myself. I have decided that the most significant thing is Grant's Tomb, right there on Riverside Drive, here in New York. Of course, most of those who are *not* New Yorkers have seen it! I do not think I ever met a born Londoner who had been in the Tower of London. And New Yorkers do not go to Grant's Tomb. They say, "He's there. He can't get away. Probably always will be there, so there's no hurry," and they never go. You should go in. There is something very extraordinary about it, and something that was quite unintentional on the part of the designers.

It is modeled obviously on the tomb of Napoleon in Paris, but it is considerably smaller. When you go into the tomb of Napoleon, there is the tomb with Napoleon, as the poet said, "alone in his glory." When you go into St. Paul's Cathedral in London, you see the tomb of Wellington and, like the warrior in the poem, there he is alone in his glory. Walk into Grant's tomb, and you see the most significant thing in America—not one tomb, but *two*. There is Grant, and there is also Mrs. Grant.

People thought that there was nothing remarkable in that. In fact, the question did not even arise in their minds. However, there is not a public monument in all of

Europe or Asia where the public man is recognized as having a wife. Of course, if you go into the parish churches in England, you will see the various lords of the manor and their wives next to them, but they are not public people. I am talking about public monuments. However, without giving it a single thought, the American people who built that monument to General Grant recognized his wife. It seemed entirely natural to them to do it and that is what makes it so significant.

Well now, just as polarity exists everywhere else, it also exists in prayer. The secret of successful prayer is to have true knowledge, fortified by feeling. If feeling alone could do it, the world would have everything by now. That is not enough. You must have right knowledge, and right knowledge is knowing that there is only One Cause. Wrong knowledge fortified by feeling keeps us in trouble, war, depression, sickness. Right knowledge, knowing there is only One Power and that the whole of the outer world is a projection of thought, saves us. Just as you cannot change the picture on the screen by rubbing the screen with a cloth, so you cannot change the world by changing the outer things. If you do not like the program at the movies, it is no use getting a cloth and rubbing the screen. You must change the reel in the projector. So to change the outer conditions, you must change your mind. You must know the Truth but you must charge it with feeling. Always there must be the father and the mother to produce the child. Neither sex alone, obviously, can become a parent. The polarity of both is required.

In the Bible, mother means the feeling nature, and the father is the knowledge nature. Most students of metaphysics, who have some understanding, have one side or the other more developed. I have known good healers who healed mostly with the father side. They knew the Truth very clearly, yet they had to have some feeling. I have known others with whom it was chiefly feeling through which they healed, but they had some knowledge too. The "father" had to be there. They knew that conditions have no power; that there is no power in matter; that there is only One Cause.

You do not have to balance these two poles perfectly but they must both be represented.

Now in this section that we have been considering, Moses represents the spiritual nature, the part of us that recognizes God as the Only Cause. His brother Aaron represents the intellect, or knowledge side, and his sister Miriam the emotional or feeling nature. They are all good in their place, but the spiritual nature has to be the leader, the master. That is the real part of you. Your physical body is only the expression. It has no power in itself for good or evil. Your physical body is just the outpicturing of the state of your emotional nature, your intellect, and your spiritual development. I do not mean that you do not have a physical body. That is foolish. Of course you have, but it is not a thing of itself. For example, some people say, "My stomach is out of order. My body is doing this to me." It is not. Your body is nothing in the world but the outpicturing of the state of your mental and spiritual makeup.

Now, all of humanity have the emotional nature awakened, most of them only too wide awake. They allow Miriam to run wild. I am using the symbology of the book of Exodus. In most people in the world, both as individuals and as nations, the emotional or feeling nature is wide awake, but it needs training. It needs purifying. It should not be destroyed or knocked on the head. The Puritans tried to do that and the fanatic ascetics tried to kill it. It has to be purified and trained. You train it by self-control, and you purify it by spiritual studies and by the search for beauty.

The intellect is much less awake in human nature as a whole. What the human race most needs today and has needed for a long time is to learn to think, to use their intellect. People sometimes come to me and say there is a great lack of love in the world or there would not be a war. No, there is not such a lack of love. Thank God that most people are kindhearted, but people do not use their intelligence. People have not taught themselves or been taught to think things through. And so humanity has to "muddle through."

Do not think that every thought you think will be demonstrated. Of course it will not. Neither will very much happen for your good if you say perfunctorily, "God is all." Fortunately, when you say negative things or when you think negative things, it does not matter particularly, so long as you do not feel them. It is every thought you feel that counts.

There are some people who sometimes indulge in what is called a temper. You know what temper is—a storm of feeling. So you see how dangerous this is. When you are very angry, or very frightened, or filled with self-pity, you are full of negative feeling, and that is the thing that is demonstrated. So watch your feelings. Miriam has to be controlled.

You can learn Truth very quickly, the father side, but the training of the feeling is the difficult thing. Train yourself to put your feeling only into the thoughts that you want to demonstrate. Keep it out of those that you do not want to demonstrate.

Suppose you are going to be angry with somebody. That is intense feeling. Now the feeling of anger is destructive, and while it may not, and usually does not, hurt the object of its anger, it is going to hurt you. If you say, "This person has behaved badly, acted meanly, deceived me, defrauded me or somebody else, but I am not going to get angry. I regret what happened, etc., etc.," the feeling is there just the same. Do not try to repress it in this way, but switch it into something that is positive. Say, "This is too bad about this person but thank God it is not I who did this thing. I can thank God he robbed me; not that I robbed him. Now he needs help. He is a human being, a child of God, the same as I am. Had I been in his shoes I might have done the same thing or worse. So I am going to save him instead of hating him. I will be angry in a moment if I am not careful so I am going to switch this into love." There is only one emotion. If used in one way it is hate; in the other it is love. There is no third. So you see the Christ in him. By doing that you have helped yourself and you will have changed him permanently.

So when our prayers fail and we do not demonstrate, we fail because we are not honoring our father and our mother. Let us have One Cause, and let us act as if we believed it. Act the part, get the thought right, fill it with feeling, and the demonstration will surely come.

CHAPTER 9

At-one-ment,
Abundance, and Adultery

*Thou shalt not covet thy neighbour's house, thou shalt
not covet thy neighbour's wife, nor his manservant, nor
his maidservant, nor his ox, nor his ass, nor any thing that
is thy neighbor's.*

EXODUS 20:17

Thou shalt not commit adultery.

EXODUS 20:14

*There was a certain man in Caesarea called Cornelius, a
centurion of the band called the Italian band,*

*A devout man, and one that feared God with all his
house, which gave much alms to the people, and prayed
to God always.*

*He saw in a vision evidently about the ninth hour of
the day an angel of God coming in to him, and saying
unto him, Cornelius.*

*And when he looked on him, he was afraid, and said,
What is it, Lord? And he said unto him, Thy prayers and
thine alms are come up for a memorial before God.*

*And now send men to Joppa, and call for one Simon,
whose surname is Peter:*

96

He lodgeth with one Simon a tanner, whose house is by the sea side: he shall tell thee what thou oughtest to do.

And when the angel which spake unto Cornelius was departed, he called two of his household servants, and a devout soldier of them that waited on him continually;

And when he had declared all these things unto them, he sent them to Joppa.

On the morrow, as they went on their journey, and drew nigh unto the city, Peter went up upon the housetop to pray about the sixth hour:

And he became very hungry, and would have eaten: but while they made ready, he fell into a trance,

And saw heaven opened, and a certain vessel descending unto him, as it had been a great sheet knit at the four corners, and let down to the earth:

Where in were all manner of fourfooted beasts of the earth, and wild beasts, and creeping things, and fowls of the air.

And there came a voice to him, Rise, Peter; kill, and eat.

But Peter said, Not so, Lord; for I have never eaten any thing that is common or unclean.

And the voice spake unto him again the second time, What God hath cleansed, that call not thou common.

This was done thrice: and the vessel was received up again into heaven.

Now while Peter doubted in himself what this vision which he had seen should mean, behold, the men which were sent from Cornelius had made inquiry for Simon's house, and stood before the gate,

And called, and asked whether Simon, which was surnamed Peter, were lodged there.

While Peter thought on the vision, the Spirit said unto him, Behold, three men seek thee.

Arise therefore, and get thee down, and go with them, doubting nothing: for I have sent them.

Then Peter went down to the men which were sent unto him from Cornelius; and said, Behold, I am he whom ye seek: what is the cause wherefore ye are come?

And they said, Cornelius the centurion, a just man, and one that feareth God, and of good report among all the nation of the Jews, was warned from God by an holy angel to send for thee into his house, and to hear words of thee.

Then called he them in, and lodged them. And on the morrow Peter went away with them, and certain brethren from Joppa accompanied him.

And the morrow after they entered into Caesarea. And Cornelius waited for them, and had called together his kinsmen and near friends.

And as Peter was coming in, Cornelius met him, and fell down at his feet, and worshipped him.

But Peter took him up, saying, Stand up; I myself also am a man.

And as he talked with him, he went in, and found many that were come together.

And he said unto them, Ye know how that it is an unlawful thing for a man that is a Jew to keep company, or come unto one of another nation; but God hath shewed me that I should not call any man common or unclean.

Therefore came I unto you without gainsaying, as soon as I was sent for: I ask therefore for what intent ye have sent for me?

And Cornelius said, Four days ago I was fasting until this hour; and at the ninth hour I prayed in my house, and, behold, a man stood before me in bright clothing,

And said, Cornelius, thy prayer is heard, and thine alms are had in remembrance in the sight of God.

Send therefore to Joppa, and call hither Simon, whose surname is Peter; he is lodged in the house of one Simon a tanner by the sea side: who, when he cometh, shall speak unto thee.

Immediately therefore I sent to thee; and thou hast well done that thou art come. Now therefore are we all here present before God, to hear all things that are commanded thee of God.

Then Peter opened his mouth, and said, Of a truth I perceive that God is no respecter of persons:

But in every nation he that feareth him, and worketh righteousness, is accepted with him.

ACTS 10:1–35

N OW these are given as two of the Commandments but I want us to consider these two together because they are different aspects of the same thing.

I have also included as a Bible reference the 10th chapter of Acts, because there is always a correspondence between the Old and the New Testaments. It is not an accident that they are bound up together. One is the unfolding of the other. If you have a Bible that gives the references in the margin, you will know, of course, that when you open the Bible anywhere, it is full of references to other parts of the Bible. Here in Exodus there are innumerable references to the Old and New Testaments, and when you turn to the Acts of the Apostles, and the Gospels, you will find the same thing. That is because the Bible is a spiritual unity. You would not have that in any secular collection of books.

In this very graphic chapter in Acts, we see that it has a bearing on the Mosaic law. It is the usual graphic picture that the Bible gives us. It takes us back to the Old World, so remote in time and place from ourselves. We see this good man Cornelius, doing the very best that he

knows, living the life according to his highest understanding. Then we see Peter, whom we know so well, and
we are given that picturesque detail—Peter was living in
a house by the seashore. Something very remarkable happened there that day. He was staying in the house of another man, also called Simon, a very common name in
those days like John or Tom with us. This Simon happened to be a tanner by trade. In the Old World they did
not have the Christian and surname as we have. A man
was known as Simon the tanner, Simon the carpenter, or
Simon the son of John, and so forth.

Peter was staying with Simon, and Peter, despite the
fact that he had followed Jesus, was still very orthodox. He
thought he was a Christian because he believed in Jesus
and used his name, just as we do. Peter is so human, so
like ourselves. We believe in Jesus and we use his name,
so we think we are Christians; but, of course, we are not,
until we have revised everything in ourselves—all our beliefs, all our prejudices, all our ideas. Most of us have
hardly revised anything since our schooldays. Most of us
have our minds made up by the time we are at school;
made up with prejudices inherited from the family, im-
bibed from the school, from the nation, from the news-
papers, and from our surroundings. We have all these
ideas. We are perfectly satisfied with them, and we never
revise them again. Oh, yes, we revise a few superficial
ideas, but not the main ones. Being a Christian, being
in metaphysics, means revising our fundamental beliefs,
and the faster we revise them the faster do we progress.

Peter had quite a lot of revising to do, and because he
constantly prayed and was absolutely sincere, his guidance came. He had this vision in which the strictest of
the Mosaic laws, the law about diet, was repealed. Moses
had taken his people out into the tropical desert and it

was necessary for him to draw up certain regulations concerning diet and sanitation. All the things in the Pentateuch (the first five books of the Old Testament), and particularly in the book of Leviticus, tell about these rules and regulations that were intended for people living in that age and in a tropical country. All kinds of ritual instruction, some under the direction of Moses and some later under the priests, are given, of what things they should eat and not eat, when they should wash, and so on. Notice that they are not in the Ten Commandments. These rituals were intended for that particular body of people, in that particular climate, and that particular time, and doubtless they were necessary, but they certainly would not apply to people living in a temperate zone in the twentieth century. They are not in the Commandments, because in the Commandments nothing is given that is not of universal and eternal application.

I am sure that it never occurred to Moses that his people would keep on doing these things slavishly for over three thousand years, or that people living in a different climate, under different conditions in crowded cities in Europe and America—so different from the Arabian Desert—would continue to do these things. I suppose if Moses came back today, he would scold his people very severely and say, "Where is your common sense? Live in the present and take the spirit of my teaching." Of course, Jesus Christ would do the very same thing if he came back today, for Christian people have done exactly what the Jews did. So have the Mohammedans and the Buddhists. We follow a leader, accept his teaching on the outside, but are either too lazy or too foolish to get beyond that into the principles that underlie it.

Well, Peter had this vision in which he was told there was nothing sacred about diet. He was to forget it and eat whatever seemed appropriate and right—at once wiping out all the artificial laws of the Pentateuch. Then he was told to mix with other people. They had been very exclusive in those days. Jews had no dealings with Samaritans. It was not a matter just of intermarrying. They avoided social intercourse of any kind. They would avoid going into the house of a Gentile to take a glass of wine socially, though there was nothing in their diet regulations concerning wine. Peter was told to stop that and meet anybody because there is no such thing as anyone being common or unclean. In other words, there is no such thing as a superior person or a superior race.

There really is no such thing as a chosen race. There never was and there never will be. No race is any better than another. The reason Moses was born a Jew instead of in another nation was because these people had kept away from idolatry and, on the whole, had kept the sanctity of their women and the purity of the home better than other nations. They had chosen God. God did not choose them.

We know there is no such thing as a chosen race. The chosen race are people anywhere in the world who seek God, and do His will. In the time that Jesus taught, the people around him were frightfully set up with themselves because they were physical descendants of Abraham. Jesus said to them, "That doesn't mean a thing. If you were really descended from Abraham, you would do as Abraham did, but you don't." The truth is that if you seek God wholeheartedly, struggle to put Him first, and carry out His will, then you are of the chosen race, one of the children of God. If you do not do that, it does not matter what race, or nation, or church you belong to. You are not of the chosen race.

It is a wonderful lesson, because we are so apt to think that because we belong to a certain nation, race, or church, it will mean our salvation. Joining a church does not mean a thing. It only means your name is on a card index for having notices mailed to you, or something like that. What else can it mean? The true chosen race is composed of those all over the world who seek God with their whole hearts and try manfully to do His will.

Jesus went up and down the country teaching people, saying in effect, "Don't imagine that because you go to the temple, go through certain ceremonies or subscribe to a certain creed, that it is going to mean anything, because it isn't. There is nothing in the world that means anything but to seek God wholeheartedly, perhaps through the valley of the shadows, perhaps on the road to Calvary, perhaps carrying a cross for some time, but seeking God through it all, and holding on."

God chooses those who choose Him. God helps those who help themselves. God turns to those who turn to Him.

The basic trouble the Jews have always had has fundamentally arisen from that feeling of their being a chosen race. As soon as you start calling yourself a chosen race, you get into trouble. Lots of Gentiles have done it too. The British did it, from about the 1850s to about 1890, until it became very tiresome, and until the Boer War brought them to their senses. Under the first Napoleon and just after, the French thought they were a chosen race. And for a time, before and during the last war, a great many Germans thought they were the superior or chosen race.

This is a terribly dangerous thing. There is not any chosen race—only those who choose God. What marks a man is his own character. The Greeks said, "Whom the gods would destroy, they first make mad," and if we really become megalomaniacs, trouble follows.

So this chapter in the Acts of the Apostles was put in to teach people that nobody is common or inferior; that there is no superior race but that one man is as good as another; and that one man has the same rights as another. After all, is that not the whole spirit and soul of our own Constitution?

Very well, now we come back to the Commandments as such. The Seventh Commandment says, "Thou shalt not commit adultery." Naturally, that Commandment means what it says. The Christian standard of conduct with regard to personal purity will never be improved on. That is the standard that has been taught by all the older Christian churches without exception. We know, of course, that purity is not the same thing as prudery. Certainly the standards of strict celibacy for unmarried people, and normal married life for married people, cannot be improved on. Now, it may seem strange to say "normal married life for married people," but it is necessary for this reason. In the past, certain religious sects and one or two sections of the metaphysical movement have taught that normal married life for married people meant living as brother and sister. That is completely wrong. Honorable marriage is entirely honorable, and it is better that married people should live a normal married life. That will not interfere with their prayers in any way. The first thing that Jesus did in public was to attend a wedding to give his approval to married life.

Now, this Commandment, "Thou shalt not commit adultery," means what it says. Not to commit adultery is fundamentally important because on it is founded the sanctity of the family. But, of course, there is a great deal more in it than that.

In the Old Testament a different form of symbolism was employed than that used in Europe and America. Our ideas and symbolism are derived, of course, chiefly from the Greeks. They are always symbols of beauty. They are always visual. For instance, to us Justice is a lady with a bandage over her eyes, and she carries a balance in her hand—a very beautiful symbol. Liberty is a lady holding up the torch of freedom—another beautiful idea. And we have our various other symbols. However, you must remember that the people of the Old Testament were forbidden to make images, and they took it literally. Moses did not want them to make statues because in that age they would have worshiped them. So he made a hard-and-fast rule, "No statues, no graven images." He did not mean that to go on forever but only for that particular generation. They had come out of Egypt where there were statues on every street corner, some beautiful, some ugly with animal heads, to be worshiped by the people. So for that generation Moses made the law, "No statues." Mohammed did the same thing long afterward for the same reason. Mohammed wanted to get his people away from worshiping statues of wood and stone, so he forbade them altogether. Moses did not intend his people to carry it on indefinitely. Incidentally, they broke it by having two statues of angels in the Holy of Holies. But there it is, human nature as usual, just as we with our knowledge of the Truth, with our knowledge of the omnipresence of God, break the Commandments every day in some way or another. And these people broke the Commandment too, but apart from that they did not make images. To them, Justice could not be a woman.

Strength could not be Hercules. Liberty could not be a woman with a torch. So they evolved a rather tortuous and, to us, sometimes an ugly symbolism.

When we read Ezekiel or Daniel, for instance, the symbolism is extremely ugly and, on occasion, quite ridiculous, because you cannot visualize it. Try to visualize chariots with many wheels and eyes, and all that sort of thing. Try to visualize a creature with six wings. Try to draw a living being with six wings. It cannot be done in a way that is not ugly. It is not visual symbolism. They used many symbols that we would not use, and some that we would consider today definitely in bad taste.

Well, one of the commonest and most used Hebrew symbols was adultery for idolatry. In the Old Testament these two words, symbolically, are almost always interchangeable. The worship of false gods was described as adultery. The soul was conceived of as the woman, and God as the husband, and when a man or woman worshiped a false god, it was described as adultery.

Now as I say, to our modern sense, that is in bad taste. We would not use that, but they did and we have to take the Bible as we find it and interpret the thing as it was written. You know that many of the Christian women mystics of the Middle Ages delighted to describe themselves as the brides of Christ. Some of the writings of these real mystics of that medieval period are not usually printed nowadays, not that there is anything definitely wrong in them, but the way they said things, to put it mildly, would be considered somewhat startling, particularly in the nice drawing rooms of suburbia. Yet they were extremely religious, devoted people. Consciously they were pure minded, but whether they were really pure minded is another matter. We understand so much about psychology nowadays that we know that when a man or woman dwells too much upon purity and such things, it is very often really repressed sex instinct.

However, the fundamental idea behind this Commandment is to have one God.

As you read through the Old Testament, the Psalms, the Proverbs, particularly the Song of Solomon, or any of the major prophets especially, you will find that the idea of the adulterous woman who is unfaithful to her husband constantly means the human soul, which is turning away to some other god. In those days it meant running after one of the heathen Egyptian or other gods. Today it does not mean that. To us it means giving power to outside things, saying, "Well now, prayer will not overcome this because of thus and so." That is giving power to a false god. "I cannot do things because I am too old," or "I haven't got money or influence," or "I can't live in this climate," or whatever it may be, is the modern form which unfaithfulness to God will take.

Now, about coveting. There are several phrases concerning this thing of coveting. You are not to covet your neighbor's house, nor his wife, nor his manservant, nor his maidservant, and so forth. Many people have thought that that was redundant because if you must not steal, that covers it. But this is a different thing. It says that you are not to covet your neighbor's house, nor his cattle, nor his wife, nor anything that is his. That is very fundamental, because very much of the evil in the world is caused by that covetousness, by wanting something to which one is not entitled.

What is jealousy? What is envy? Is it anything but covetousness? When we look at some other man or woman and we wish that we had something that is his, to which we are not entitled in justice, we are coveting, and that is terribly bad for us—and Moses knew it. Moses, I think, knew more about the human heart than anyone who has ever lived except Jesus. He knew what covetousness does to us in, what we call today, the unconscious or the sub-conscious, and so he stressed it in the literal and old-fashioned Oriental way.

The best literary taste today feels that emphasis should be gotten by incisive or powerful statement. It is only very unsophisticated people who resort to many italics, be-cause many italics on a page result in a loss of emphasis. We prefer, in our modern way, to give emphasis by strength or incisiveness of expression. In the Old World, they piled things up. They said, "Thou shalt not covet thy neighbor's house, nor his wife, nor his manservant, nor his maid-servant," piling up this law that we must not covet.

If you see something that somebody else has and you like it and you think that you would like to have the same, that is fine. But do not want to take it away from him, and do not hate him because he has it and you have not. As a matter of fact, no one has anything that does not come direct from God. God's supply is infinite, and the very thing that your neighbor has, God has an infinite amount of and will be glad to give it to you if you will furnish the consciousness through which it can appear. Now you may say, "Well, that is absolutely true, but it is rather obvious." No, I am afraid it is not obvious at all. It is so little obvious that it has been causing trouble in the world for thousands of years before Moses was born and ever since then. It is the whole cause of the trouble in the world today, covetousness on all sides.

There is not any nation, at least not one of the big ones, that has not coveted other people's possessions and helped itself to them when it could. The tragedy is that the little fellows, little countries like Holland, Belgium, and Finland, who have never threatened anybody, or been any danger—quite decent, clean, orderly, honest, God-loving people—get into trouble that has been brought about by the covetousness of other nations, some in the twentieth century, some in the nineteenth century, and some in the eighteenth. So you see this thing of coveting other people's property and other people's good is not unimportant. If it had been unimportant, Moses would not have stressed it so.

Now we modern civilized people, as individuals, do not go about coveting actual goods. We do not say, "Well, now, Jones next door has an ox, and I wish I had that." To begin with, Jones usually does not have an ox, in most parts of Europe and America, but he has an automobile, or a radio, or a refrigerator. Yet we do not covet these things, as a rule. I do not think anyone says, "I wish I had Jones' Ford or Cadillac." We are too grown up for that. We do not really covet possessions like that. However, we do covet the supply that makes it possible for him to have them. We are going home perhaps to our own modest apartment. We pass a very attractive house and we covet the supply that got it for that man. We may not put it quite like that but we covet his job, or his knowledge, or his education, or his influence, or his personality, and that is rather deadly.

But on the whole, I do not think that individuals covet so much nowadays, but whole nations do covet other nations' possessions. One nation, for instance, will covet the oil wells of another. One nation says, "We have no oil. Other people have it, and we need it." They covet it. Or they covet another nation's rubber or tin, or what you please. So they invade that country to get them. Of course, the invasion is often done under quite another pretext. The South African Boers, a very excellent people, were living quietly in their country, farming, but they had the misfortune to have gold and diamonds deposited there in the ground. Other people coveted the diamonds and the gold, and war followed.

Coveting leads to aggression, theft, murder, but that is not the worst of it. The worst of it is that it affects the soul of man. Even if your coveting never leads you to take anything that does not belong to you, it undermines and ultimately rots your soul. It shuts you off from God. Why? Because to covet something means that you do not understand the Law of Being. You do not understand that you cannot steal. You do not understand that whatever you are getting or lacking is the outpicturing and expression of your consciousness. Until you understand that you cannot be saved.

Until men and women understand that nothing can ever happen to them—that nothing can ever come to them or be kept away from them—except in accordance with the state of their consciousness, they do not have the key to life and they cannot be saved.

How can you be saved if you do not know the law? Until you realize this truth, which is on every page of the Bible, that it is your state of mind that matters, that it is your state of mind that puts you into that house, or into that job—or walking the street without a job, or that gives you a sick body or a well body; that it is your mind and your consciousness that rule your life; then there is no hope for you. You do not have the key to life.

And so whether coveting is a very wicked thing or not in itself, the fact is that to covet means that we are missing the key to life. When you see somebody else in possession of something that you think very nice and very desirable, that is fine. Admire it, but say to yourself, "I am in touch with the Source of that. The lovely house that he has, her happy marriage, his wonderful position, I am in touch with the Source of that. God's supply is inexhaustible, and I can have the same and better." And it is sure to be better because what fits the other fellow would not suit you exactly. If you took it from him it would not fit, but the thing you get from God will fit perfectly.

Now you see that these two ideas, coveting and adultery, are really bound together because coveting is disloyalty to God and so, in the Old Testament sense, it is adultery; and when the Bible says not to commit adultery, it means not to worship some other God. If you think you can only get what your neighbor has by taking it from him, you are worshiping a false God.

There is not anything in the world that you ever conceived of or dreamt of that God has not got in abundance in the realm of archetypal ideas. You know that the sun shines on the earth and everybody can have as much sunshine as he wants. If everybody in the United States, on a summer's day, went sunbathing from Canada to the Gulf of Mexico and from the Atlantic to the Pacific, there would be enough sunshine for all, and no one would go short. You would not get less because the man in the next yard was sunbathing too.

So it is with all of God's supply. It is infinite, and to envy someone else because he has a better position, or seems to have more, is to deny your own contact with God. It is to say, "The only way I can get this is to steal," and we have seen that we cannot steal.

Moses knew all these things, and if we realize them in the spirit in which Moses meant them, not being narrow or pedantic, but taking the true spiritual meaning, then we shall have the key to life.

CHAPTER 10

Seven Steps to Fulfillment

> *Remember the sabbath day, to keep it holy.*
> *Six days shalt thou labour, and do all thy work:*
> *But the seventh day is the sabbath of the Lord thy God:*
> *in it thou shalt not do any work, thou, nor thy son, nor*
> *thy daughter, thy manservant, nor thy maidservant, nor*
> *thy cattle, nor thy stranger that is within thy gates:*
> *For in six days the Lord made heaven and earth, the sea,*
> *and all that in them is, and rested the seventh day: where-*
> *fore the Lord blessed the sabbath day, and hallowed it.*
>
> EXODUS 20:8–11

W E now have reached the end, for the time being, of our study of the Commandments, and we come to this Commandment about the Sabbath Day. I kept it until the end because it is perhaps the one that is most misunderstood, or shall I say, least understood. I am sure some of you are going to be shocked. I hope so. I always think that a sermon in which I shock no one is a wasted opportunity. But I hope and trust I have never preached such a sermon. Until and unless

112

we are shocked out of our complacency, we never are ready for the new interpretation.

This Commandment was given to the people at the time of their leaving Egypt, and going into the desert, and on the surface it meant what it said for that age.

Now, of course, the Sabbath Day came once a week, and that was a very obvious arrangement because it followed the phases of the moon. The ancients always used the lunar month. They had a good deal of knowledge of astronomy, but they did not have our knowledge, for instance, that the earth goes around the sun (with the exception of a very few advanced students, but it was not generally known). The moon was the important thing, and the phases of the moon split the month up into four sections. So the seventh day was a natural time, and one day in seven seems to fit human personality and human psychology.

Other systems have been tried. During the French Revolution for a short time under Robespierre, the French followed the tenth day. Robespierre and some of the intellectuals around him—his brain trust—went crazy on the decimal system, and so people had to wait for the tenth day to get a day of rest. And some people tried the fifth day, but knocking off from work every fifth day meant that work was really neglected and caused confusion. One day in seven seems to be the natural and reasonable time.

It was a wonderful thing in Moses' day to insist that everybody set aside one day a week to think about God and about religion, or at least to oblige him to stop his secular activities. No rule made by Moses, no law made by Parliament or Congress or anyone else can make a man religious, or make him spiritual and give him faith, but it can help. And so this law at least made it compulsory that everybody should have a day of rest—even the slaves. There were very careful attempts made by Moses to regulate slavery, but still there was slavery or bondage. And so under this Commandment their owners or employers were obliged to give them one day off a week. That was as far as the law would go, and they were enjoined to give that time to God. That was a great advance. In the old civilizations the privileged people, the instructed people, used to have their time of rest, but as a rule the mass of the people were under bondage in all those countries, and they did not.

But here was a law that applied to those in authority as well as to the humblest man or the poorest slave or serf or bondsman. They were all given the right to turn to God.

Notice that this Commandment does not say that the leaders of the people, the more important sections, shall keep the Sabbath Day, but everybody, and Moses emphasizes this in the Oriental way by saying neither your son, nor your daughter, nor your manservant, nor your maidservant, nor the stranger within your gate, shall do any work on the Sabbath. That was the best way of driving home to those people the importance of the individual, the sacredness of the individual.

Incidentally, that idea is the idea that runs through the whole of the American Constitution. I hope everybody has read it recently. Many people read it at school or high school and then never think of it afterward. The whole idea is based from beginning to end on the importance, the dignity, the sacredness of the individual, and all the provisions in the Constitution and the Bill of Rights are attempts to safeguard that. Under totalitarianism, no matter what we may call it, there is a complete denial of the dignity, and rights, and sacredness of the individual. He is only a cog in a wheel, a creature of the State—the State meaning whatever man has placed himself in power.

So among other things this Commandment gives the opposite idea, and it teaches the sanctity of the individual.

Now we saw that Moses had found these people living in Egypt, a highly civilized, sophisticated country, a very pagan and idolatrous country, very corrupt morally, and that while many of the Jews were simple, laboring people, quite a number of them had done very well and had gone into the professions, and occupied important positions. He had to take them out into the wilderness and keep them there for more than a generation, so that those who were brought up in Egypt would pass on and the people who would start the new way of life would be the people born in the desert. Moses did that because it is very hard to change us. As the old lady said, "We are sot in our ways," mentally, and we do not like to change. We imbibe prejudices in our younger days and, as a rule, we never get away from them. The only way to get away from them is to have the spiritual experience of a contact with God, and most people will not take the trouble to get that. They want God, certainly, if they can get Him easily, but they will not pay the price of heart-searching, of a change in conduct, change in outlook, revising both their ideas and their conduct.

So Moses, who knew human nature so well, said, "I will take them into the wilderness, and train the new generation, and take them into the Promised Land to start the new civilization." Consequently, he made a rule that they must stop working one day a week, get together and be preached at, and taught and lectured to, and generally instructed. He arranged that that should be the seventh day, which we call Saturday. We call it Saturn's day, or Saturday. The Old Testament calls it the Sabbath.

Moses was writing laws for his people, and he was also, as we saw in previous chapters, writing a metaphysical treatise that would give the Truth of Being to anyone who was ready for that, in Moses' time or after. The general public had to be trained simply, and those who were further advanced needed something more. Every teacher has found that. Jesus said to his disciples, "Feed my lambs, feed my sheep." The lambs are the beginners, the general public, the young spiritually; the sheep are the more mature and understanding people, those who are more advanced spiritually. Paul speaks of milk for babes, and meat for men. Let me put myself, and Paul, right with the vegetarians by saying that he did not mean flesh meat alone, but food in general.

Moses meant the same thing, and for the lambs, those young in spiritual understanding, he arranged for the seventh day to be kept. But an extraordinary thing happened. As the centuries went on, the great prophet came, the greatest of all, Jesus Christ, came, and he told his people that these laws were all right for the time of Moses, but that they had to revise them, reconsider them, and live in their own age; not to make a superstition of the Sabbath or anything else. That frightened many of them. People in the time of Jesus were very much like us. They wanted to stick to the things they were accustomed to, because they were emotionally committed to them, and they did not have the spiritual courage to break away.

Jesus said, "Moses said thus and so, but I say unto you . . . ," and the people answered, "Oh no! Moses said it all and there is no right to add or subtract anything from what Moses said." But Jesus did not think so. He constantly says, "Moses said . . . but I say unto you. . . ." In particular, he said that the rigid Sabbath-keeping activities since Moses' time had become a mere superstition; thus he made a point of doing anything necessary on the Sabbath Day, and the stupid people who would not think for themselves, hypocrites and humbugs, used that as a lever against him.

He healed a man on the Sabbath. He met a poor creature who was in agony, had been sick for years, and had lost all hope. Jesus met him, and because Jesus could read thought directly, he saw that this man was ready for the Truth. This sick man was not a clever fellow. He was not an intellectual man, he was not a saint, he was not an important person—just a poor sick nobody—but he had the right heart. Jesus saw it and so he healed him. All the hypocrites who hated Jesus and were jealous of him said, "Oh! You healed a man on the Sabbath Day!" And Jesus answered them suitably.* Even his immediate followers, having been brought up in the old tradition, found difficulty in tearing themselves away.

In the previous chapter we read about Peter's vision, how he was shown that the dietary laws of Moses were no longer valid, that he did not have to avoid certain foods. As Jesus said, it does not matter what you eat. That is not important spiritually. It is what you think. The inspired writers put this in the Gospel so clearly that nothing but the average thoughtlessness of people could miss it. Jesus put it simply and clearly. It is not what goeth into the mouth that defileth a man—it is not what you eat that matters to your soul—it is what cometh out of the

---

* John 5.

mouth, the words you speak, or the thoughts you think, that make the difference.*

The early Christians broke away from the Sabbath idea; but time went on, and, strange to say, Christians who did not have the excuse of being brought up in the old law—the Gentile Christians, not the Jewish Christians—took over the Hebrew Sabbath, but they changed the day. They said in effect, "We will keep the Sabbath, but we will keep it on the first day of the week." And every Jew with a sense of humor (and I have never known one who had not) just laughed. They said, "These poor foolish people. They think they are keeping our Sabbath, and they are doing it on Sunday, the first day of the week."

Down through the ages, people (particularly the Puritans) went on keeping Sunday under the impression that the Jewish law was binding on them, when all the time the Jewish law says that the Sabbath is Saturday.

There was a time in Scotland when you could be put in jail for whistling on Sunday. I have heard some whistlers—and crooners—that should be put in jail any day of the week, although not on religious grounds! But that is by the by.

You know what the Puritans did about Sunday in New England. There has never been a greater piece of folly in the world than the Puritan Sabbath because if the Jewish laws were binding at all, they should have observed Saturday. Of course, it was simply a refusal to think, to work out their beliefs to their logical conclusion.

If you imagine that by just abstaining from work on Sunday you are going to save your soul, you could not make a greater mistake. An idle Sunday is of no more

---

* Matthew 15:11, 19, 20.

spiritual value than an idle Thursday or Tuesday. To think so is superstition.

Years ago in London I knew a man who was a good and sincere man, very intelligent in a general way, and he said to me, "I have had a lot of trouble in my business. For some time it has been going to pieces. This thing has happened; that thing has happened; and I can't understand it, because ever since I have been a child I have kept Sunday most rigorously." He was perfectly sincere. He continued, "Two or three times in my life I have had offers of a lot of money, but the position entailed working on Sunday and I had to refuse." He had done what seemed to him the right thing. Yet all these troubles had happened to him. Actually he was a good, sincere, kindly man, making a one-sided agreement with the Almighty, which could not mean anything. In effect, he said to God, "Look here, I won't work on Sunday no matter how much I am offered. On the other hand, You will take care of me." No meaning at all, not the slightest. If that man wanted his business to prosper the only way was to think rightly about his business. And I happen to know that he was not businesslike in his ways. He was sincere and honest, but he was not very intelligent in his business methods. He could not make up for that by doing or not doing something on a particular day of the week. So this man was really guilty of superstition although his intentions were so good. The only way to have his relations with other people right was to know the Truth about his fellow man, by seeing the Christ in him. If he had wanted his health and the other phases of his life to be harmonious, the only way was to think rightly about them.

Whatever you think rightly concerning, will go well. Whatever you think wrongly concerning, will go ill. You

can prove it for yourself. Take some particular department in your life. Treat it with true thought for several
weeks, and you will be amazed at what will happen.

What does this particular Commandment mean? Like
all the Commandments, when we analyze them, it is instruction in metaphysical truth and scientific prayer. By
scientific prayer we mean seeing the presence of God everywhere, particularly where the error seems to be—
building up the right thought about it.

The way to change your thought about a thing is to
take that thing into your prayers. Remind yourself of the
omnipresence of God. Make it clear, make it real to yourself, realize that God is present where the trouble seems
to be, that what you see as a material activity is a spiritual activity and must be right and true. The foreign
thoughts that come in, foreign to God and Truth, such
as thoughts of fear, doubt, inadequacy, opposition, competition, and so forth, must be handled by supplanting
them with the thought of the goodness and love of God.
Remind yourself that God can and does supply your every
need. Where there is fear and doubt He brings faith,
where there is lack He brings abundance, and so forth.
Build up the new consciousness in this way—and then
let it alone. That is the Sabbath Day. If you constantly
keep opening the treatment to add something else, as it
were, there is no Sabbath Day. In any kind of mental work
that you do, you must have a Sabbath. "Six days shalt
thou labour. . . . But the seventh day is the sabbath of the
Lord. . . . in it thou shalt not do any work."

Now it may take you a year to get to that stage, or you
may do it in ten seconds. If it is an easy problem for you
to solve and you are a quick thinker, you may do the
whole seven days in a few minutes. If it is an obstinate

problem, it may take a year. But always the seven days of creation are the time that it takes to create a new condition in your life—a healing, or harmony in some personal relationship.

It is also true for the negative things we make, the ailments, the physical difficulties we bring upon ourselves by our wrong thinking. The difficulties and problems we get into by acting or speaking unwisely—they take "seven days" to complete too. Sometimes a person, for example, will overwork for five years before his health suffers. Another time, a man or a woman will talk himself or herself into very serious trouble by five minutes' conversation at the wrong time. In both cases it is the seven days of creation.

Now the mystical meaning of seven is personal perfection. Each of these numbers in the Bible has a mystical meaning, not a prophetic one. The Bible does not give prophecy of what is going to happen in detail to the human race, because that would mean that we have no free will, and that prayer meant nothing. But the numbers have a mystical meaning, and seven stands for personal perfection. And so it means that we must set aside a time for God in accordance with our personal need.

In the seven days of creation in Genesis, to which Moses refers here, we are told that God rested from his labors on the seventh day. I do not suppose that any person of the slightest intelligence nowadays, at any rate in the Western world of Europe and America, really believes that God is a big man who worked with his hands like a man, made this universe, and then after working for six days was a little tired, like a human being, and had to rest. That was the old-fashioned, literal interpretation. Obviously that is not true. It is an allegory. The seven days of Genesis* are allegorical. Actually, the world as we know it is created by the human race all the time. The world is the outpicturing of human thought. For generations human thought has been filled with fear and distrust, a sense of separate nations, and that is eventually outpictured as war.

The world is what we make it by our thinking. It was not made by God in six days. God did not make the lions and the tigers, and then all kinds of deadly germs, and snakes, and so forth. That world is the outpicturing of our thought. This concept may shock some people, but, as I said, I hope I never preach a sermon that does not at least shock some people.

Now, to accomplish any work you need a Sabbath Day. If you cannot let a thing alone when you have done it, it cannot grow. I often speak of the child who plants a bulb and digs it up every day to see how it is getting along. Of course, there will be no flower.

You know if you make a pudding or a pie, and put it into the oven, you have to let it alone. First, you work to make it. (A year or two ago I was taken to task because I was foolish. I described the making of a cake in detail, and because I put lard in my cake I heard about it.) At any rate, you make your cake. You spend some time on it. You get the ingredients, flour, fruit, etc., and you put them together. You have made your cake. That is the six days. Then you put it into the oven and leave it. Inexperienced people keep opening the oven door to see how things are getting on, and you know that ruins the cake.

So it is with any activity. If you watch a skillful man at work, or the work of a technician who knows his job plan-

---

* See "The Seven Days of Creation" in *Alter Your Life*, p. 34.

ning something, you will always find the Sabbath Day.
He does his work and then leaves it. With the bungler
or the amateur, there is no Sabbath. He is at it all the
time and the thing never works out properly.

It is true in prayer and it is true in any kind of healing. There is a time for work and there is a time for rest.
I know not how many people there are in this metaphysical movement who miss their demonstration because they are praying so hard and so constantly that
there is no Sabbath.

Take, for example, the body. Everything that happens
to your body is the outpicturing of some fear or some
belief in the mind, usually subconscious. Sometimes these
things are prenatal. You brought them over with you
from a previous life. It does not at all follow that if you are
laid up, it is owing to some present fear or false belief. It
may be something out of the past, but they are there.
However, nothing can appear upon the body that is not
first in what we call the unconscious or subconscious
mind.

The subconscious mind, you see, is very important—
and good, by the way. We could not even walk across the
floor without it. Learning to walk, for example, was training the subconscious. The subconscious is not bad. However, there are a lot of things in the subconscious that
are bad, and it is our business to get them out. We have
to redeem the subconscious, and that is what our salvation is.

The subconscious has always worked for us. It is the
oldest part of us, and it works with symbol and allegory.
That is why dreams are always allegorical. You never
dream of the person that you think you dream of. It is
symbolizing something for you.

So when things happen to the body that you do not expect, they are always in the subconscious mind first. Therefore, there is not anything that happens to the body that the mind cannot heal. The practical difficulty is to get it to do so. Nevertheless, there is nothing in your body that your mind cannot change. It can heal up lesions. It can get rid of growths, so that they drop away. I have seen that happen.

I saw a very interesting case myself in London a few years ago. There was a young girl who used to attend New Thought meetings—I saw her several times—who had a very ugly growth on her forehead, over the eye, nearly as big as a plum. It did not bother her but it was very ugly. It was what doctors would call a cyst, I presume. One day a teacher came along to London, who had that power that some people have to inspire others with confidence in God. Some teachers tell us about it but they do not always give us that confidence. However, this man had the genius of making people really feel and believe that God in them could do anything. It was a small drawing-room meeting of twenty-five or thirty people. After the talk he walked around among the people sitting there, and this girl said to him, "Could I do anything about this?" He said, "Why not? You heard what I have been saying. Of course, you can." Well, about three days later she came into the meeting, and it was gone. I saw that myself. It was gone, and she told us that that morning she found it on her pillow. It had fallen off in the night. The skin was a little pink, as new skin is, and that soon went away.

I had some conversation with her, because I have always been from Missouri, although I did not know it until I came to New York! I have never swallowed anything I have been told without evidence, not that I disbelieve people, but I like to be shown. There was no question about this healing. I talked to the girl to get some idea of what she was like, and found that she was a simple Cockney girl, with no education, goodhearted, honest, but not particularly bright. We will let it go at that, which meant that she had no intellectual pride, no spiritual pride. She was not too clever. She probably had no training of any kind, but she was obviously simplehearted—and it is to the simplehearted people that God comes.

There is nothing in the world that shuts us off from God like being too smart. That was the sin of the Pharisees, the only people of whom Jesus was intolerant. A Pharisee was a fellow who thought he was rather smart. He knew all about it before he heard it. You know the wonderful story of the Pharisee and the publican. One man knelt at the back of the temple and said, "God have mercy on me, a sinner." The other walked right up to the front and said, "O God, I am thankful that I am not like this poor publican here. I am a very good fellow. I carry out all the laws. I go to church regularly. I am an advanced metaphysician," and all that sort of thing. Jesus told that story and a child could not miss its import.

This particular incident I mentioned to you concerning the healing of the girl is an illustration of this. The wisest man in the country, the most learned man, could get a healing just as quickly as that girl, if he were as open for it.

Too often, however, a little knowledge is a dangerous thing, and we think we know too much to learn more. That is intellectual pride, and its twin brother, spiritual pride. If we want to experience God, if we want healing and harmony in our lives, we have to follow the rules of Jesus. He understood this subject better than anyone else who ever lived, and he said that to enter the kingdom of heaven we must become like a child. He was childlike

himself in many ways, not childish but childlike. Jesus
was the wisest man who ever lived. He knew more about
human nature than anyone else before or since. He knew
all about God and the constitution of the universe, but
there was a childlike quality in him. He had no intellectual pride, and, of course, no spiritual pride. He went
straight to God with his prayers. We waste so much time
on third-rate religious rubbish, I am afraid I must call it,
that too often we overlook the prayers of Jesus. He went
straight to God. There was a simple, childlike quality and
yet one that was immensely profound. Of all the people
who ever lived, Jesus loved mankind the most. I wonder
when humanity will learn that lesson, that the secret of
life, life here and life eternal, is in divine love. There is
not anything higher than that.

The last thing that the Bible says about God directly
is that God is love. When shall we learn that? We have
been so trained in fear in the past—trained in fear because it is so much easier, so much quicker at least, to
handle people by fear than it is to handle them by love—
that we are slow to learn that God is love. But that is the
key to life. The most powerful prayer is the prayer of the
person who has the most love. Every atom of fear, or condemnation, or criticism, that we carry in our hearts, no
matter for whom it may be, is a wall between ourselves
and God.

The shortcut to the presence of God is to fill our hearts
with divine love for everybody, particularly people or
things we do not like. The shortcut to power in prayer
is to fill our hearts with divine love. The shortcut to happiness is to fill our hearts with divine love. The sure and
certain way to overcome fear is to empty the heart of fear
by filling it with love, because if we are filled with love, as

Jesus was, of what should we be afraid? Jesus was without fear. The devil came—the devil means the race mind—and found nothing in him because his heart was filled with love.

We can measure our progress in spiritual things, not by outer conditions, but by the extent to which we are getting rid of hatred, criticism, and condemnation. The yardstick by which we can measure spiritual progress is the degree to which our hearts are filled with unselfish and undemanding love.

However, we must remember that in all spiritual work, there must always be a Sabbath. Jesus said, "Unless a seed go into the earth and die, it cannot come up." That was his way of saying that we should make our prayer, do our spiritual work, and then rest from our labors, so that the demonstration can come to fruition. That is our Sabbath of the Lord. That was the teaching of Moses and that is the teaching of Jesus, and it never can be surpassed.

Now, I have said two or three times that there are several layers of meaning in the Commandments, and here in this Commandment about the Sabbath Day there is a still deeper meaning.

When you are praying every day and recognizing that God is working in you and in all your affairs, and trying to live the spiritual life, then something else will happen. There will be a sense in which every day will be a Sabbath, because for you every day will be a holy day.

One of the most wonderful things about the Jesus Christ teaching that we call metaphysics today is that we get rid of the distinction between the sacred and the secular. Of all the things that our study of the Bible and spiritual truth does for us, one of the greatest is that it wipes out the distinction between the secular and the sacred.

That is one of the most important steps in the whole history of the soul.

You are going to live forever somewhere. I do not say where. I do not know, but you are going to live forever somewhere, and in the course of your history there will never be a more important step than that. There are several steps of primary importance and this is one of them. You have made a fundamental step forward in your spiritual life the day that you realize—not the day you first hear of it—the day you realize that no longer for you is there any difference between the secular and the sacred, because you are realizing that everything that happens is the expression of God, that everything that has any real existence is His expression. You have then realized what immanence means, which was the name the old mystics gave to it, meaning the omnipresence of God—that God exists everywhere and in all things, that everything that exists is the expression of God. Not evil, because evil has no existence in reality. Evil is our false beliefs and misinterpretations concerning God and his manifestation.

The Ninth Symphony was the expression of Beethoven. If one sits down and plays it wrongly, that does not alter the Symphony. Our interpretation was wrong. Now the whole of your manifestation—your body, your home, and your surroundings—is the expression of God in you, although you *may be* misinterpreting it, and if you are having difficulties, you *are* misinterpreting it, and the healing is to interpret it correctly. The day that you can realize and know that God is all there is, that there is no difference between the secular and the sacred, that all things are sacred, that will be one of the greatest milestones in your whole history, and then it will always be the Sabbath Day for you. When you know that you will understand what

God meant when He said to Moses, "The place whereon thou standest is holy ground."

You will realize that a temple or a church is a convenient building in which people can worship God together and remind themselves of holy things, but that God is just as present out in the streets, out in the fields, in the factory, in the office, and in your own home. You could sit in the most beautiful church in the world, and have mean thoughts and thus bring trouble upon yourself; and you could sit in a jail or a poorhouse, and have thoughts of peace and harmony, although if you did that you would not be there very long.

God is present everywhere, and that is the meaning of the Sabbath Day in its deepest sense. For those who understand the metaphysical teaching, it is always the Sabbath Day, and the place whereon they stand is holy ground.

CHAPTER 11

Every Problem Has a Solution

And it came to pass, that, while Apollos was at Corinth, Paul having passed through the upper coasts came to Ephesus: and finding certain disciples,

He said unto them, Have ye received the Holy Ghost since ye believed? And they said unto him, We have not so much as heard whether there be any Holy Ghost.

And he said unto them, Unto what then were ye baptized? And they said, Unto John's baptism.

Then said Paul, John verily baptized with the baptism of repentance, saying unto the people, that they should believe on him which should come after him, that is, on Christ Jesus.

When they heard this, they were baptized in the name of the Lord Jesus.

And when Paul had laid his hands upon them, the Holy Ghost came on them; and they spake with tongues, and prophesied. . . .

And he went into the synagogue, and spake boldly . . . concerning the kingdom of God. . . .

And this continued by the space of two years; so that all they which dwelt in Asia heard the word of the Lord Jesus, both Jews and Greeks.

And God wrought special miracles by the hands of Paul. . . .

Then certain of the vagabond Jews, exorcists, took upon them to call over them which had evil spirits the name of the Lord Jesus, saying, We adjure you by Jesus whom Paul preacheth.

And there were seven sons of one Sceva, a Jew, and chief of the priests, which did so.

And the evil spirit answered and said, Jesus I know, and Paul I know; but who are ye?

And the man in whom the evil spirit was leaped on them, and overcame them, and prevailed against them, so that they fled out of that house naked and wounded.

And this was known to all the Jews and Greeks also dwelling at Ephesus; and fear fell on them all, and the name of the Lord Jesus was magnified.

And many that believed came, and confessed, and shewed their deeds.

Many of them also which used curious arts brought their books together, and burned them before all men: and they counted the price of them, and found it fifty thousand pieces of silver.

So mightily grew the word of God and prevailed. . . .

And the same time there arose no small stir about that way.

For a certain man named Demetrius, a silversmith, which made silver shrines for Diana, brought no small gain unto the craftsmen;

Whom he called together with the workmen of like occupation, and said, Sirs, ye know that by this craft we have our wealth.

Moreover ye see and hear, that not alone at Ephesus, but almost throughout all Asia, this Paul hath persuaded and turned away much people, saying that they be no gods, which are made with hands:

So that not only this our craft is in danger to be set at nought; but also that the temple of the great goddess Diana should be despised, and her magnificence should be destroyed, whom all Asia and the world worshippeth.

And when they heard these sayings, they were full of wrath, and cried out, saying, Great is Diana of the Ephesians.

And the whole city was filled with confusion: and having caught Gaius and Aristarchus, men of Macedonia, Paul's companions in travel, they rushed with one accord into the theatre.

And when Paul would have entered in unto the people, the disciples suffered him not.

And certain of the chief of Asia, which were his friends, sent unto him, desiring him that he would not adventure himself into the theatre.

Some therefore cried one thing, and some another: for the assembly was confused; and the more part knew not wherefore they were come together.

And they drew Alexander out of the multitude, the Jews putting him forward. And Alexander beckoned with the hand, and would have made his defence unto the people.

But when they knew that he was a Jew, all with one voice about the space of two hours cried out, Great is Diana of the Ephesians.

And when the townclerk, had appeased the people, he said, Ye men of Ephesus, what man is there that knoweth not how that the city of the Ephesians is a worshipper of the great goddess Diana, and of the image which fell down from Jupiter?

Seeing then that these things cannot be spoken against, ye ought to be quiet, and to do nothing rashly.

For ye have brought hither these men, which are neither robbers of churches, nor yet blasphemers of your goddess.

Wherefore if Demetrius, and the craftsmen which are with him, have a matter against any man, the law is open, and there are deputies: let them implead one another.

*But if ye inquire any thing concerning other matters,
it shall be determined in a lawful assembly.*

*For we are in danger to be called in question for this
day's uproar, there being no cause whereby we may give an
account of this concourse.*

*And when he had thus spoken, he dismissed the as-
sembly.*

ACTS 19:1–41

T HIS is a very striking chapter, an extremely col-
orful and dramatic chapter even for the Bible,
which is so full of color and drama. I cannot
understand why so many people with literary tastes neglect the Bible today. It was not so a generation ago. One
good thing I can say for the Victorians is that they did
appreciate the literary beauty of the Bible. I suppose that
is the principal reason why they wrote so well. They often
talked nonsense but they wrote remarkably well.

In Victorian days, both in America and England, many
of those writers who often did not believe in religion at
all, still kept the Bible on their tables and read it every day
for the beauty, the drama, and the color of its literature.

And here in this chapter we are carried back into the
old Oriental world, a world of confusion and change,
much like our world today. These people come alive to us.
Demetrius, the silversmith, Paul and the others, we know
better than many we meet in daily life; and we see that
while they all professed some kind of religion, in their
hearts they said, "Great is Diana of the Ephesians," because to them Diana stood for the outer things—the
things they did not want changed. Even those who thought
they were Christians said, "Well, we have never even heard
of the Holy Spirit," and in their hearts, although they did

not say it with their tongues, they too acted the thought, "Great is Diana of the Ephesians."

The subject of this chapter is that every problem has a solution, and that is really what the Ten Commandments tell us and that is also the Jesus Christ message. Every problem has a solution. There is no difficulty that can come to you or me for which there is not a solution and for which we shall not find a solution in time, if we persevere. Some problems last a long time, some a short time, but always there is a solution, and *always the solution is to turn from the outer to the inner.*

Now in this light I want us to review what we have been considering about the Ten Commandments, because an understanding of what is given in the Ten Commandments is the solution to any problem, no matter what your problem may be. It may be a material problem. It may be a spiritual problem. It may be a physical problem. It may be a problem of personal relationships. But the solution to that problem is found in the understanding of what we call the Ten Commandments.

In the form in which we have them they constitute a chart to the sea of life, and whether your problem is a big one that intimidates you, or a small one that annoys you, the solution is in the understanding of these Commandments.

Well now, the First Commandment says, "I am the Lord thy God. . . . Thou shalt have no other gods before me." That is the first, and you know that always the beginning is half the battle. Always try to make a good beginning, and if you do not, scrap things and start again.

In the old occult tradition the most important thing was always put first. So the First Commandment says, "I am the Lord thy God. . . . Thou shalt have no other gods before me"; and all our troubles ultimately arise from breaking

the First Commandment, because the First Commandment sums up the ten. It is very characteristic of the Old
World way of writing that they give us a series—eight
beatitudes, ten commandments, the eightfold path, and
so forth—and that later ones are really a commentary
on the first.

So "I am the Lord thy God" is the first and greatest of
the Commandments, and all your troubles really arise
from neglecting this and saying, "Great is Diana of the
Ephesians"—looking at the outside either in admiration
or in fear. When you admire some outer, passing thing too
much, and thus give power to the manifestation, you are
saying, "Great is Diana." When you fear some outer thing
or condition or person, then you are also saying, "Great
is Diana." And when you say, "Great is Diana," then your
troubles really begin.

Now, Diana of the Ephesians happened to be a symbol of idolatry. The worship of Diana is no worse than
that of many other pagan gods. Because she was a Greek
goddess, she was beautiful. Most of the Egyptian and
Chaldean gods were very ugly, Dagon and the others,
but the ancient Greeks always did things beautifully. However, the fundamental trouble in our lives is just this. We
do not know whether there be a Holy Spirit or not, and
we shout, "Great is Diana."

Why did the intelligent Greek people—these were not
the classical Greeks, of course; the Greeks of that day
were intelligent but lacking in what we call character—
why did they shout, "Great is Diana!"? Well, because in
their hearts they thought it meant their bread and butter. It was not disinterested enthusiasm for Diana, but it
meant, as they thought, their livelihood, their bread and
butter, their life. When we worship outside things, it is
because we too are afraid of what may happen if we lose

them, whereas our one and only salvation is just to lose them. The only salvation for man is that he shall lose his belief in outer things and if there is no other way, they must be taken from him by force. If we really withdraw our belief from the outer thing and place it upon God, we need not suffer. As a rule, we will not do that. It is only when the outer thing is torn from us that we will let go, and because it is better to lose Diana at any cost than to lose God, it is well that that should happen.

The First Commandment is, "I am the Lord thy God"— God, Spirit, nothing outside. There is not a single mistake that you or I have ever made, there is not a single trouble or heartache that has ever come to us, that has not come directly through breaking this Commandment, through saying, "Great is Diana," and forgetting God. We can dodge it. We can fool ourselves. We can say our troubles came from something else. We can even say our troubles came because we were too noble or too good. But that is not true. Our troubles always come because we have forgotten God and have shouted, "Great is Diana."

So it says, "I am the Lord thy God," and then it says, "which have brought thee out of the land of Egypt, out of the house of bondage." Some people say they believe in God, but they do not think anything can come of it, and even that it is not nice to expect it. They say, "These people who expect God to give them healings, pay the rent, give them their bread and butter, and everything else—it's very vulgar." But the Bible does not agree with them. On the contrary, it says, "I am the Lord thy God"— Who does things, Who takes care of you—Who brought you out of the land of Egypt and out of the house of bondage.

And then it says, "Thou shalt have no other gods before me"—no Diana—and, "Thou shalt not make unto thee any graven image, or any likeness," and so forth. That is the Oriental way of stressing that point. The Bible uses all the stress that it can command to tell us that we are not to have any kind of idol or graven image. That is the Bible's way of saying, "Don't make an idol of a person, a business, an investment, some position of honor or glory, or anything that you can think of." Diana of the Ephesians takes many forms. Many a man has lost his soul, at least temporarily because you cannot lose it permanently—the soul is God—he has lost his sense of God through what to others would seem a totally inadequate reason. So the Bible says, "Look around and see if you are making an idol of something." And then it says, "Thou shalt not bow down thyself to them, nor serve them." When you allow a thing to frighten you, you are bowing down to it.

It is perfectly true that if you walked into a museum and saw a statue of Diana, you would not grovel before the image, but the only reason is because it is not fashionable. When you are afraid of anything you are worshiping it. Whatever you fear, you bow down to. So when you let yourself be scared by the front page of the newspaper, or by what is happening in the stock market, whether it is going up or down, you are bowing down and worshiping an idol.

And then the Bible says, "I am a jealous God," and we saw that that was Moses' way of saying God must have first place. You can have other things in your life but God must be first. He will not play second fiddle. That does not mean God is a jealous individual, but it does mean that unless you put the presence of God first, you will lose God altogether. That is the Law of Being, and the universe is a universe of law. It is a universe, not a chaos. You know perfectly well that if you want electric light, you must have a proper circuit. If you have ever developed a photograph, you know that if you want it to come out successfully, you must keep the film away from the light until it is fixed. It would not matter who you were. If you say, "I'll let the light in for just a minute. I won't count that," you will destroy the whole thing. Even if you say, "This is very important. It's for Mr. So-and-so," it will not make the slightest difference. You must keep the law. The supreme Law of Being is that God must be first in your life. Anything that conflicts with doing what we believe is His will must go. He must have first place.

And then it goes on and says, in substance, that you cannot take the name of the Lord in vain. You cannot. Now people think that they are only taking the name of God in vain when they use His name. You know how, from time to time, we are shocked by hearing people use the name of God in a disrespectful way; and most of us do not like to hear the name of Jesus Christ used lightly or disrespectfully. It is a peculiar sidelight on human nature that quite often people who consider themselves pious will use the name of God in an improper manner. I leave that with you in passing.

Actually you use the name of God whenever you believe in something. What you really believe in is your God. What you really believe in you are attributing to God. What you really believe in you are expressing as God. That is your idea of God. If you believe in some limitation, you are limiting God. Your beliefs are your expressions of what you think about God. And so when you believe in limitation, you are saying God is limited. You are denying His Godhood. Now, whatever you believe in is going to happen to you, not the things you think you ought to believe in, not the things you say—we often say what we think is correct, what we think is expected—but it is what you really believe in that happens to you.

For instance, we really believe in age. We really believe in the calendar. We really believe, we can say what we like, but most of us really believe that every year we are 365 days older—except leap year, when we are 366 days older! And so people age as per schedule, and take on from the race mind the ills and ailments that go with that age. Some people look a few years younger than the calendar says and some look a few years older. That is the only difference. When we cease to believe in that, we shall cease to manifest it.

We cannot take the name of the Lord in vain. We cannot believe in something and not have that happen to us. If we only knew that! If that could only be taught every child—because it is so simple a child could learn it! A normal child of ten years of age could understand that. You cannot take the name of God in vain. What you really believe in will happen to you, and you cannot avoid it. Therefore, it is important that you see to it that you believe in the goodness, and mercy, and love, and omnipresence of God.

And then the Bible says, "Keep the Sabbath Day holy." We must not make a superstition of Sunday. I do not mean that it is not a good thing to have one day a week off. I do not want to abolish Sunday. I think it is an excellent thing to have one day a week set aside for relaxation and rest and recreation. That was not the idea, for instance, of the Puritans. They made a superstition of it. Why did a Puritan New Englander in the nineteenth century refuse to do anything, even sometimes to ride in a horsecar, on Sunday? Why did he refuse to do any work on *Sunday* at all? Because the ancient Hebrews were told not to do any work on *Saturday*. That was the logic of it. If the Hebrew Sabbath were binding on the Puritan, then he should have had kosher food and all the rest of it. So let us not make a superstition of that. Let us thank God for Sunday.

It is a splendid habit to go to church on Sunday, but go to church because you want to worship God with other people, community worship, and because you want to learn something. Do not go to church as a sedative. That is superstition.

The real meaning of that Commandment is instruction in prayer. The fundamental or basic meaning of all Bible teaching turns out to be instruction in prayer, because that is the only activity that matters. There is nothing else that really matters. You say, "Oh yes, I can do other things. I can eat, drink, buy, sell, and so forth." No, these are your acts. They are only expressions of your character.

Right now you are a certain person, a certain character. You know what a character is. It is a bundle of habits with a customary outlook. That is what you are. That bundle of characteristics in some respects is much better known to your family than to yourself. They have mentioned it to you from time to time, I am sure! But parts of it are known only to you. However, right now you are a certain person, and all you can do, apart from prayer, is to act that part. You can only be yourself, apart from prayer. If you are honest, you cannot steal, but if you are a light-fingered person and if an opportunity arose—someone left a purse or a watch around—you could not resist it. You might have made many good resolutions, but they would do you no good. A thief might say, "I have been inside [meaning in prison]. I'm not going back there again." But there is the watch, the purse, the money, and he must do it because he is a thief. If you are a kind-hearted person, you must say or do something kind when there is an opportunity. If you are a mean person, you cannot resist saying something that will hurt. And all the king's horses and all the king's men cannot do anything about it. If you are efficient, you must work efficiently, but if you are a bungler, and if the firm gave you the finest equipment, you would bungle away. You must do what you are, *except by prayer,* and then that changes you. If the thief prays, he becomes honest and cannot steal. If the mean man prays, kindness of heart breaks out. He cannot say those mean or unworthy things. And if the stupid man or the bungler prays, he becomes wise and efficient and cannot spoil things ever again.

So prayer is the only activity, and the great thing for prayer is to pray your prayer, give your treatment as we say in metaphysics, and then let it alone. That is keeping the Sabbath. Do not keep nibbling at it. When tomorrow comes, pray again if necessary. Do not say, "This will do for today. Tomorrow I will have another go at it," because that is saying that the prayer you have just finished is not good enough. It is like a man praying for fine weather who takes an umbrella just in case. Pray, and believe your prayer is going to work. Act the part. Leave it.

Then it says, "Honour thy father and thy mother: that thy days may be long upon the land." We know the underlying meaning of that is that the knowledge and the feeling side, the intellect and the emotions, have to be balanced. "The land" in the Bible means manifestation. To have your days long in the land means that you will have power over your surroundings. It means that you can heal your body or that of others, control your business life, make your home happy, and so forth, and to do that, you must balance the knowledge and the feeling side.

Now, the knowledge side is easier for most people. The knowledge side consists in understanding that God is the only power, and if you give any power to anything apart from God, you are limiting God. If you say, "We can't heal that because the man is too old," or if you say, "I could succeed in California, but I can't in New York," that is denying God. It is really shouting, "Great is Diana," and you will not get anywhere. But when you understand that God is not limited by conditions, that it does not matter how sick you are today, what mistakes you have made, how foolish you have been, or how strong the forces against you seem to be—God is stronger than conditions—that is the knowledge side.

The world thinks that the so-called laws of nature—in which I believe in their place on this plane—are true right up to the heart of God and cannot be changed. However, we know that if you rise above the physical plane in consciousness, you can change them, but while you are on the level of the physical plane, you are under their control. The world thinks that a man of this age cannot be healed as easily as a man of that age. The world thinks some diseases are easy to heal while others are impossible to cure. The world thinks if you take certain problems in time, you can overcome them, but that if you do not, you cannot. However, we know that it is never too late because God is outside of time. So we have the knowledge side.

What most of us lack is the feeling half. Our feelings are given over to the side of fear. The more feeling you have, the stronger your emotional nature, the better, if you throw it on the positive side, but the worse, if you throw it on the negative side. It is like a high-powered car that can easily do a hundred miles an hour. That is fine, if you are on the right kind of special roadway, like the Pennsylvania Turnpike. However, if you are a bad driver and get into the car lightheartedly and step on the gas, that car is going to wreck you. Emotional feeling is like that. Throw it on the good side, on the side of Divine Love, believe in God, believe in yourself, believe in the future, believe in harmony, and it will drive you right out of any trouble. However, too often human nature throws it on the other side, the side of ifs and doubts and buts and fears, and, of course, it suffers.

And then there are a few people who become so cold-blooded, so superior, and so withered with spiritual pride that they have no feeling at all. They turn up their noses at the world and say how advanced they are, and they punish themselves very severely.

So if you leave out one of these two sides, you are not honoring your father and your mother, and you will not have any real power in prayer.

Then the Bible tells us that you cannot kill anything. The consciousness must express itself for what it is, good or bad, and you cannot kill it in the outer. You can change your consciousness by prayer, but you cannot kill it.

That gives us the key to changing our lives for the better. We can bring into our lives any good we want by working first in our consciousness and changing that by prayer and meditation. As the consciousness changes, the change in the outer will follow from that.

Then we saw that "Thou shalt not commit adultery" is extremely and fundamentally important in its surface meaning because of the necessity for keeping the sanctity of the family. And we also saw that "adultery" in the Old

Testament is often used interchangeably with "idolatry," and that means "No Diana!" In the Old World the soul was constantly thought of as being the bride of God. God is the bridegroom and the soul of man is the bride. Whenever you give power to anything besides God, you are making an idol of it, and making idols brings its own retribution. We can solve many of our problems by ceasing to shout, "Great is Diana!" and giving full allegiance to God.

Then we saw that you cannot steal. You cannot have anything that does not belong to you by right of consciousness. You can appropriate what does not belong to you for the time being, but it will not stay with you, and it will bring great suffering and grief. Emerson says, "Nothing can permanently deny its own nature," and "We surround ourselves with the true image of ourselves." These are other ways of putting the same idea. You cannot steal because you cannot keep what does not belong to you by right of consciousness. Conversely, what is yours by right of consciousness, no one can take from you. Any good that you desire in your life, you must first build into your consciousness.

The next Commandment says that you must not bear false witness, and we saw that its true meaning, its inner meaning, was that it is our duty to demonstrate as the glorious sons of God, to regenerate in body, mind, and soul. Between you and me, none of us is doing it completely as yet, but we know it is our duty, and I think we are going to do it before very long, because man is beginning to revise his ideas about God and man and the universe. I have great hopes for the human race. I know that the shadow of death and destruction and hatred that is hanging over the world is going to go. Men and women everywhere are going to live together in mutual respect and toleration.

Then the last Commandment, "Thou shalt not covet," really sums up the other nine because it teaches that the outer must correspond to the inner. If you wish abundance or any good thing, you must have it in your consciousness first, because the outer will always correspond to the inner. Although Moses gave this Commandment some eleven or twelve hundred years before Jesus Christ, it also sums up the Sermon on the Mount because Jesus came and took it and amplified it. The whole teaching of Jesus is that the outer is but the result of the inner. As you believe, so do you express.

If you want peace, harmony, love, abundance, and health in your life, then you must begin by changing the inner, and the way to do that is to *believe* that God is working through you. Quietly turn to Him, and claim that He is guiding, strengthening you, opening your way. Quietly believe it. That is the secret of life, and that secret will open any door, bridge any gap, remove any obstacle, retrieve any mistake, shut out any sin, and clear up any grief, because it is claiming and realizing His Presence, and in His Presence is fullness of joy.